DEFINING MOMENTS
McCARTHYISM
AND THE
COMMUNIST THREAT

DEFINING MOMENTS
MᶜCARTHYISM
AND THE
COMMUNIST THREAT

Kevin Hillstrom

P.O. Box 31-1640
Detroit, MI 48231

Omnigraphics, Inc.

Kevin Hillstrom, *Series Editor*
Cherie D. Abbey, *Managing Editor*

Peter E. Ruffner, *Publisher*
Matthew P. Barbour, *Senior Vice President*

Elizabeth Collins, *Research and Permissions Coordinator*
Kevin M. Hayes, *Operations Manager*

Allison A. Beckett and Mary Butler, *Research Staff*
Cherry Stockdale, *Permissions Assistant*
Shirley Amore, Martha Johns, and Kirk Kauffmann, *Administrative Staff*

Library of Congress Cataloging-in-Publication Data

Hillstrom, Kevin, 1963-
    McCarthyism and the communist threat / by Kevin Hillstrom.
        p. cm. — (Defining moments)
    Includes bibliographical references and index.
    Summary: "Provides an absorbing overview of Senator Joseph McCarthy and his anti-Communist "witch hunts" of the 1950s. Also explores the ways in which the McCarthy era shaped the trajectory of American politics and culture for decades to come. Includes a narrative overview, biographies, primary sources, chronology, glossary, bibliography, and index"—Provided by publisher.
    ISBN 978-0-7808-1184-3 (hardcover : alk. paper) 1. Anti-communist movements--United States--History--20th century--Juvenile literature. 2. McCarthy, Joseph, 1908-1957--Juvenile literature. 3. Legislators--United States--Biography--Juvenile literature. 4. United States. Congress. Senate--Biography--Juvenile literature. I. Title.
    E743.5.H53 2011
    973.918--dc22   2010051244

Printed in the United States of America

TABLE OF CONTENTS

NARRATIVE OVERVIEW

BIOGRAPHIES

PRIMARY SOURCES

PREFACE

Throughout the course of America's existence, its people, culture, and institutions have been periodically challenged—and in many cases transformed—by profound historical events. Some of these momentous events, such as women's suffrage, the civil rights movement, and U.S. involvement in World War II, invigorated the nation and strengthened American confidence and capabilities. Others, such as the Great Depression, the Vietnam War, and Watergate, have prompted troubled assessments and heated debates about the country's core beliefs and character.

Some of these defining moments in American history were years or even decades in the making. The Harlem Renaissance and the New Deal, for example, unfurled over the span of several years, while the American labor movement and the Cold War evolved over the course of decades. Other defining moments, such as the Cuban missile crisis and the Japanese attack on Pearl Harbor, transpired over a matter of days or weeks.

But although significant differences exist among these events in terms of their duration and their place in the timeline of American history, all share the same basic characteristic: they transformed the United States's political, cultural, and social landscape for future generations of Americans.

Taking heed of this fundamental reality, American citizens, schools, and other institutions are increasingly emphasizing the importance of understanding our nation's history. Omnigraphics's *Defining Moments* series was created for the express purpose of meeting this growing appetite for authoritative, useful historical resources. This series will be of enduring value to anyone interested in learning more about America's past—and in understanding how those historical events continue to reverberate in the twenty-first century.

Each individual volume of *Defining Moments* provides a valuable resource for readers interested in learning about the most profound events in our nation's history. Each volume is organized into three distinct sections—Narrative Overview, Biographies, and Primary Sources.

- The **Narrative Overview** provides readers with a detailed, factual account of the origins and progression of the "defining moment" being examined. It also explores the event's lasting impact on America's political and cultural landscape.

- The **Biographies** section provides valuable biographical background on leading figures associated with the event in question. Each biography concludes with a list of sources for further information on the profiled individual.

- The **Primary Sources** section collects a wide variety of pertinent primary source materials from the era under discussion, including official documents, papers and resolutions, letters, oral histories, memoirs, editorials, and other important works.

Individually, each of these sections is a rich resource for users. Together, they comprise an authoritative, balanced, and absorbing examination of some of the most significant events in U.S. history.

Other notable features contained within each volume in the series include a glossary of important individuals, places, and terms; a detailed chronology featuring page references to relevant sections of the narrative; an annotated bibliography of sources for further study; an extensive general bibliography that reflects the wide range of historical sources consulted by the author; and a subject index.

New Feature—Research Topics for Student Reports

Each volume in the *Defining Moments* series now includes a list of research topics, detailing some of the important topics that recur throughout the volume and providing a valuable starting point for research. Students working on essays and reports will find this feature especially useful as they try to narrow down their research interests.

These research topics are covered throughout the different sections of the book: the narrative overview, the biographies, the primary sources, the chronology, and the important people, places, and terms section. This wide coverage allows readers to view the topic through a variety of different approaches.

Students using *Defining Moments: McCarthyism and the Communist Threat* will find information on a wide range of topics suitable for conducting historical research and writing reports.

Acknowledgements

This series was developed in consultation with a distinguished Advisory Board comprised of public librarians, school librarians, and educators. They evaluated the series as it developed, and their comments and suggestions were invaluable throughout the production process. Any errors in this and other volumes in the series are ours alone. Following is a list of board members who contributed to the *Defining Moments* series:

Gail Beaver, M.A., M.A.L.S.
Adjunct Lecturer, University of Michigan
Ann Arbor, MI

Melissa C. Bergin, L.M.S., NBCT
Library Media Specialist
Niskayuna High School
Niskayuna, NY

Rose Davenport, M.S.L.S., Ed.S.
Library Media Specialist
Pershing High School Library
Detroit, MI

Karen Imarisio, A.M.L.S.
Assistant Head of Adult Services
Bloomfield Twp. Public Library
Bloomfield Hills, MI

Nancy Larsen, M.L.S., M.S. Ed.
Library Media Specialist
Clarkston High School
Clarkston, MI

Marilyn Mast, M.I.L.S.
Kingswood Campus Librarian
Cranbrook Kingswood Upper School
Bloomfield Hills, MI

Rosemary Orlando, M.L.I.S.
Library Director
St. Clair Shores Public Library
St. Clair Shores, MI

Comments and Suggestions

We welcome your comments on *Defining Moments: McCarthyism and the Communist Threat* and suggestions for other events in U.S. history that warrant treatment in the *Defining Moments* series. Correspondence should be addressed to:

Editor, *Defining Moments*
Omnigraphics, Inc.
P.O. Box 31-1640
Detroit, MI 48231
E-mail: editorial@omnigraphics.com

HOW TO USE THIS BOOK

Defining Moments: McCarthyism and the Communist Threat provides users with a detailed and authoritative overview of the rise and fall of Senator Joseph McCarthy—and the impact of the phenomenon known as McCarthyism—on the politics and culture of the United States. The preparation and arrangement of this volume—and all other books in the *Defining Moments* series—reflect an emphasis on providing a thorough and objective account of events that shaped our nation, presented in an easy-to-use reference work.

Defining Moments: McCarthyism and the Communist Threat is divided into three primary sections. The first of these sections, the **Narrative Overview**, explains the origins of American fears about Communism, traces the arc of Communist activism in the United States in the first half of the twentieth century, and examines the Cold War factors that intensified anti-Communist sentiments across the country. It also details the political rise of Senator Joseph McCarthy, reviews the impact of his investigations on American politics and society, and chronicles the events that drove him to his ultimate defeat and disgrace. The section concludes with a discussion of McCarthyism's lasting impact on U.S. politics and culture.

The second section, **Biographies**, provides valuable biographical background on Joseph McCarthy and other individuals associated with the rise of McCarthyism, including Roy Cohn, J. Edgar Hoover, and Martin Dies. Profiles are also presented, however, of several Americans who famously opposed McCarthy, including Edward R. Murrow and Joseph N. Welch. Each biography concludes with a list of sources for further information on the profiled individual.

The third section, **Primary Sources**, collects essential and illuminating documents from the McCarthy era. Selections include excerpts from the

House Un-American Activities Committee testimony of Alger Hiss and Whittaker Chambers; the 1950 speech in West Virginia that launched McCarthy to political stardom; Margaret Chase Smith's "Declaration of Conscience"; Edward R. Murrow's *See It Now* special on McCarthy; the Army-McCarthy hearings that doomed McCarthy; and an Arthur Miller essay on the creation of his anti-McCarthyism play *The Crucible*.

Other features in *Defining Moments: McCarthyism and the Communist Threat* include the following:

- A list of Research Topics that provide students with starting points for research.

- Attribution and referencing of primary sources and other quoted material to help guide users to other valuable historical research resources.

- Glossary of Important People, Places, and Terms.

- Detailed Chronology of events with a *see reference* feature. Under this arrangement, events listed in the chronology include a reference to page numbers within the Narrative Overview wherein users can find additional information on the event in question.

- Photographs of the leading figures and major events associated with the development and growth of McCarthyism.

- Sources for Further Study, an annotated list of noteworthy works about the McCarthy era.

- Extensive bibliography of works consulted in the creation of this book, including books, periodicals, and Internet sites.

- A Subject Index.

RESEARCH TOPICS FOR
DEFINING MOMENTS: MCCARTHYISM AND THE COMMUNIST THREAT

Starting a research paper can be a challenge, as students struggle to decide what area to study. Now, each book in the *Defining Moments* series includes a list of research topics, detailing some of the important topics that recur throughout the volume and providing a valuable starting point for research. Students working on essays and reports will find this feature especially useful as they try to narrow down their research interests.

These research topics are covered throughout the different sections of the book: the narrative overview, the biographies, the primary sources, the chronology, and the important people, places, and terms section. This wide coverage allows readers to view the topic through a variety of different approaches.

Students using *Defining Moments: McCarthyism and the Communist Threat* will find information on a wide range of topics suitable for conducting historical research and writing reports:

- The impact of the Russian Revolution of 1917 on American politics.

- Communism's increased popularity in the United States in the 1930s, when business closures, mass unemployment, and other elements of the Great Depression were at their peak.

- The advent of the Cold War and its effect on party politics in America.

- The creation and development of the House Un-American Activities Committee (HUAC), Congress's leading anti-radical investigative body during the 1940s.

- Political, social, and economic factors that contributed to divergent views about the relative threat posed by Communism among the mid-twentieth-century U.S. populace.

- The trials of Alger Hiss, the most famous accused spy in U.S. history.

- Ways in which Senator Joseph McCarthy's relationship with the press helped him accrue political power in the early 1950s.

- The complex and strained relationship between McCarthy and the administration of fellow Republican Dwight D. Eisenhower.

- The "Red-baiting" tactics of McCarthy and their impact on American society.

- Lessons and legacy of McCarthy era on future generations of Americans.

NARRATIVE OVERVIEW

PROLOGUE

⊰⊷∩⊶⊱

When U.S. senator Joseph Raymond McCarthy woke up on the morning of February 9, 1950, few Americans knew who he was. To be sure, most voters in the state of Wisconsin recognized the name, for they had been the ones who sent McCarthy to Washington a little more than three years earlier. Since that time, though, McCarthy had not distinguished himself among the 100 members of the U.S. Senate. Many other senators had more seniority than McCarthy. Journalists who wanted the perspective of a conservative Republican like McCarthy on the Cold War, the threat to America posed by the Communist regime of the Soviet Union, or other pressing issues of the day recognized that there were far more famous and influential lawmakers who they could interview.

On February 9, however, McCarthy set in motion a series of events that would make him the most feared and controversial politician in America. Over the next three and a half years, in fact, the junior senator from Wisconsin emerged as the nation's most famous crusader against Communist spies and sympathizers in America. But in the process, he stoked fear, distrust, and dissension to unprecedented levels in countless American neighborhoods and communities. Within months of his rise to prominence, the nation was in the grip of what came to be known as "McCarthyism"—a phenomenon in which huge numbers of Americans were accused of being traitors to their country on the basis of nonexistent or distorted evidence.

How did the fortunes of McCarthy—and the United States—change so dramatically in the course of a single day? Because that afternoon McCarthy delivered an historic speech in Wheeling, West Virginia, to a small gathering of Republican women on the threat posed to America by Communism. Most of McCarthy's remarks merely repeated points that the audience had heard many times before. But in mid-speech he made a startling claim:

As one of our outstanding historical figures once said, "When a great democracy is destroyed, it will not be because of enemies from without but rather because of enemies from within." The truth of this statement is becoming terrifyingly clear as we see this country each day losing on every front.

At war's end we were physically the strongest nation on Earth and, at least potentially, the most powerful intellectually and morally. Ours could have been the honor of being a beacon in the desert of destruction, a shining, living proof that civilization was not yet ready to destroy itself. Unfortunately, we have failed miserably and tragically to arise to the opportunity.

The reason why we find ourselves in a position of impotency is not because our only powerful, potential enemy has sent men to invade our shores, but rather because of the traitorous actions of those who have been treated so well by this nation. It has not been the less fortunate or members of minority groups who have been selling this nation out, but rather those who have had all the benefits that the wealthiest nation on earth has had to offer—the finest homes, the finest college education, and the finest jobs in government we can give.

This is glaringly true in the State Department…. In my opinion the State Department, which is one of the most important government departments, is thoroughly infested with communists. I have in my hand 57 cases of individuals who would appear to be either card-carrying members or certainly loyal to the Communist Party, but who nevertheless are still helping to shape our foreign policy.[1]

This statement—and most especially his declaration that he *possessed the names* of actual Communist traitors operating in America—made McCarthy a household name virtually overnight. And once McCarthy strode into the public spotlight, America was forever changed.

Notes

[1] McCarthy, Joseph. Speech to Women's Republican Club, Wheeling, West Virginia, February 9, 1950. U.S. Senate, State Department Loyalty Investigation Committee on Foreign Relations, *Congressional Record*, 81st Congress, Second Session, February 20, 1950, p. 1956.

Chapter One

EARLY AMERICAN FEARS ABOUT THE "RED MENACE"

> My one desire is to acquaint [the American press] with the real menace of evil-thinking which is the foundation of the Red movement.
>
> —U.S. attorney general A. Mitchell Palmer, January 27, 1920

At various turbulent periods in the history of the United States, large numbers of Americans have become convinced that the nation's prosperity—and even its very existence—was under attack from radical enemies within. For much of the twentieth century, one of the nation's deepest fears was that legions of Communist agents had infiltrated American society and government as part of a plot to destroy the American way of life. This anxiety is most closely associated with the 1950s, when Senator Joseph McCarthy conducted his infamous Communist "witch hunts." But the fear of Communist infiltrators actually emerged in American homes more than three decades earlier, and it cast a shadow over the nation right up to the outbreak of World War II.

Nativism in the Nineteenth Century

Ever since the founding of the United States in 1776, a belief has persisted among many citizens that the nation and its most cherished traditions and principles need constant protection from wicked or inferior people capable of destroying the state. During the second half of the nineteenth century, when millions of immigrants from all over the globe poured into America in search of new freedoms and opportunities, this fear became particularly intense. Some native-born Americans saw these immigrants—or certain ethnic groups among them, at any rate—as a threat to their way of life rather than a poten-

This artist's rendering of the Know-Nothing Party's "ideal" American citizen was published in 1854. The portrait of "Uncle Sam's Youngest son" is framed by patriotic symbols including an American flag and an eagle with a shield.

tial source of added strength and vitality for the young nation.

This attitude of hostility toward new immigrants (especially those with unfamiliar customs or languages) came to be known as nativism. Its primary characteristics included distrust of the morality and capabilities of unfamiliar foreigners, and a corresponding conviction that American social and economic policies should be crafted in ways that favored the interests of "real Americans" rather than the newcomers. However, white people of western European heritage who held nativist beliefs generally excluded Native Americans and African Americans from their circle of "real Americans," even though people from these ethnic groups had lived on American soil for many generations (and in the case of Native Americans, long before any white Europeans set foot on the North American continent). In fact, nativists frequently regarded blacks and "the red man" as potential threats to the security and stability of the European-style society they were building out of the forests, prairies, and mountains of America.

A wide range of peoples who came to the United States during the 1800s were victimized by bigoted, fear-fueled campaigns of nativist aggression. Jews, Catholics, Chinese, Italians, and immigrants from eastern Europe all felt the wrath of the nativists at one time or another. Perhaps the most famous of these crusades against the foreign "alien," though, occurred in the 1840s and 1850s, when the so-called Know-Nothing movement took aim at Irish Catholic immigrants.

The Know-Nothings arose as a force in American politics beginning in the mid-1840s, when native-born Protestant Americans of western European descent became alarmed by the massive numbers of Irish Catholic immigrants that were fleeing their famine-stricken native country for America's shores. Concerned that the Irish would eventually overrun the United States, nativists in New York State responded by forming an anti-immigrant secret society called the Order of the Star-Spangled Banner.

In its earliest days, leaders of the society instructed all members to answer any questions they received about the organization by saying "I know nothing." These instructions became the basis for the widely used Know-Nothing nickname even after the group threw off its mantle of secrecy in the early 1850s and waded into the world of American politics. The Know-Nothings agitated for strong new immigration restrictions, deportation of foreign-born paupers, and laws to keep Catholics from holding public office. Convinced that America's purity was being corrupted by Irish Catholics (and other immigrants who did not hail from western Europe), they blamed labor unrest, urban crime, problems within Protestant denominations, and many other complex issues on the immigrant "riffraff" in their midst. The most radical members of the group insisted that Roman Catholics from Ireland and elsewhere were plotting to take over the United States and install the pope as its ruler.

For a brief period of time, the Know-Nothings threatened to become an enduring force in U.S. politics. The group, which changed its official name to the American Party in 1854, managed to attract almost a million members by the mid-1850s. This explosive growth enabled it to make a big splash in the 1854 elections. The Know-Nothings' unyielding nativist message attracted large numbers of voters—enough for the party to claim more than 100 seats in the U.S. Congress, governorships of eight states, control of the Massachusetts legislature, and mayoral victories in major cities like Boston and Philadelphia.

These triumphs provided a major boost to the Know-Nothings, who framed their bigotry as a holy mission. "The grand work of the American party is the principle of nationality," proclaimed a leading Know-Nothing journal in 1855. "We must do something to protect and vindicate it. If we do not it will be destroyed."[1] As it turned out, however, the issue of slavery split the American Party down the same regional lines that were dividing the nation as a whole. In late 1855 the Know-Nothings ruptured into Northern abolitionist and Southern pro-slavery wings. One year later the party's presidential candidate, Millard Fillmore, managed to gain only 23 percent of the popular vote. The party dissolved quickly after that, with many of its former members eventually drifting into the ranks of the new Republican Party.

Calls for Social Justice Bring Backlash

From the end of the Civil War to the close of the nineteenth century, the United States experienced more than three decades of breathtaking but turbulent growth in virtually every measurable category. The economy soared to new heights during this so-called "Gilded Age" on the strength of the Industrial Revolution and American-style capitalism. The nation also expanded to the Pacific Ocean, sprouting new farming, logging, mining, and ranching operations every step of the way. And its population spiraled ever-upward, driven by gradual improvements in life expectancy and the continued influx—despite grumblings from nativists—of hopeful immigrants.

Many Americans rode these waves of change to better lives. And as they became accustomed to their more comfortable and secure stations in life, many of them became steadfast defenders of the evolving American society that made those new and improved lives possible. But not all people benefited from the tumult of the late nineteenth century. To the contrary, millions of native-born and immigrant workers and their families struggled for survival on a daily basis. For the men and women who toiled long hours for low wages in underground mines, dangerous factories, and steaming fields—and who had no choice but to raise their children in squalid urban tenements or drafty rural shacks—America's so-called Gilded Age offered no relief from the grinding struggle for life's basic necessities.

The stark contrast between rich and poor sparked strong objections from critics who claimed that American society could—and should—do more to ensure social justice and equality. Both the Populist Movement of the late nineteenth century and the Progressive Movement of the early twentieth century addressed pressing economic and social problems that disadvantaged the most vulnerable members of American society. During this same era, unions of organized workers formed in many industries. All of these early labor unions demanded higher wages, better working conditions, and other changes to America's capitalist system. But some of the most radical organizations, most notably the Industrial Workers of the World (IWW), viewed violence and vandalism as legitimate weapons to be used in their campaigns against the powerful companies that sat atop America's major industries.

The reform spirit of the Progressive Era led to demonstrations such as this 1909 anti–child labor parade in New York City. Both of the banners seen here—one in English and one in Yiddish—refer to child labor as "slavery."

Reformers also assumed a higher profile in the world of American politics during these decades. Most reform-minded politicians, officials, and activists operated within the framework of the mainstream Progressive Movement, which wanted to improve—not dismantle—America's basic economic and political foundations. But some were attracted to more radical left-wing movements such as socialism and anarchism, which called for a complete restructuring of American society and its institutions.

Americans responded to these calls for reform with caution and skepticism. They generally agreed that some issues highlighted by the reformers, such as the use of child labor by industry, needed to be addressed. But many other calls for reform were met with doubt or anxiety by ordinary Americans, especially because the most radical critics of American life got the most attention from newspaper and magazine writers, business and religious leaders, and politicians. Indeed, industry executives, conservative lawmakers, and other opponents of reform worked furiously to paint the most radical critics as representative of the entire reform cause. Union organizers, socialists, and even mainstream progressives thus came to be seen by some Americans as troublemaking subversives who threatened the nation's stability.

Constitutional Rights under Attack

In 1917 the United States entered World War I, a conflict that roiled Europe from 1914 to 1918. Once President Woodrow Wilson made the decision to go to war, his administration and supporters in Congress and the nation's great newspapers launched a determined campaign to organize public support for the war effort. One of the main strategies they employed was to silence left-wing opponents of the war. They accomplished this goal by imposing new restrictions on freedom of speech, even though the First Amendment to the Constitution explicitly prohibits Congress from making any such law.

The Espionage Act of 1917 made it illegal for anyone to use spoken or written language to interfere with the war effort or military recruitment. One year later, an amendment to the Espionage Act known as the Sedition Act made it a felony to use, verbally or in print, "disloyal, profane, scurrilous, or abusive language about the form of government of the United States … or by word or act oppose the cause of the United States" during wartime. Essentially, these laws made it illegal for American citizens to criticize the U.S. government during wartime.

These laws were denounced by opponents of the war ranging from Socialist leader Eugene Debs to IWW organizer William "Big Bill" Haywood. Both Debs and Haywood even received prison sentences for violating the acts (although Haywood fled the country to avoid prison). But when critics challenged the laws in court, the U.S. legal system sided with the Wilson administration. And the criticisms of the Espionage and Sedition Acts failed to make a dent in the American public's support for the measures. Convinced that the war critics were undermining American society from within, the public decided that sacrificing some civil liberties was acceptable in order to silence them.

The Great Red Scare

At the same time that perceived enemies of the state were being targeted by the Espionage and Sedition Acts, a huge historical event was taking place halfway around the world. The bloody Russian Revolution of 1917 tore down the ruthless Tsarist monarchy that had long controlled Russia and replaced it with a Bolshevik government led by Vladimir Lenin. The Bolsheviks, who eventually became known as Communists, quickly installed a political system based on state ownership of property and the creation of a classless society. In addition, Lenin and his followers proclaimed their deep hatred of America's political, economic, and social institutions.

This attitude was on full display in March 1919, when an organization called the Communist International, or Comintern, was formed in Moscow. Comintern was founded to encourage and coordinate revolutionary Bolshevik activity in other countries. It bluntly called for a "workers' revolution" that would overthrow capitalist governments around the world and replace them with Communist models. Three years later, Russia enlisted several neighboring republics that also had turned to Communism to form the Union of Soviet Socialist Republics (USSR), also known as the Soviet Union.

The rise of Vladimir Lenin to power in Russia in 1917 triggered America's first Great Red Scare.

The rapid turn of events in Russia stunned Americans from all walks of life. Their concerns about this new threat further intensified as U.S. newspapers and magazines published distorted or unsubstantiated stories about Lenin and the new Communist regime. "It was claimed that the Soviets had an electric guillotine that chopped off hundreds of heads an hour; Bolshevik leaders drove around in fancy automobiles while businessmen were starving to death," wrote historian David Oshinsky. "Most Americans believed these stories. They were frightened by Bolshivism and puzzled by its success. To their thinking, it could be categorized as the direct antithesis of everything for which America stood."[2]

Longtime critics of American business and society, from mainstream liberal progressives to radical socialists and unionists, suffered mightily in this heightened environment of fear and uncertainty. Conservative lawmakers, businessmen, and activists now claimed that these reformers were little more than Bolsheviks in disguise—and that their "solutions" to America's social and economic problems would send the nation hurtling down the path of Communism. These charges were accepted or given serious consideration by large numbers of Americans who wanted a return to the peaceful and uneventful lives they had enjoyed before the war, the Bolshevik Revolution, and domestic "agitators" had created so much upheaval. "Most Americans simply got frightened and looked for the villains … who had destroyed the nice comfortable world of 1914," wrote scholar John Roche. "The simplest answer, one which fit neatly into a long tradition of nativism, was to blame foreign influence, and specifically the impending conquest of Americans by foreign radicals."[3]

The 1918 Sedition Act made it a felony to use "disloyal, profane, scurrilous, or abusive language about the form of government of the United States … or by word or act oppose the cause of the United States."

American fears about domestic treachery and disloyalty further escalated in 1919 and 1920. In late April 1919 authorities intercepted dozens of mail bombs intended for prominent business leaders, judges, and public officials known for their anti-labor, anti-immigrant, or anti-radical stances. Less than two months later, eight U.S. cities were rocked by larger bombs that again were aimed at judges and public officials (the bombs killed several innocent bystanders but failed to kill any of their intended targets). Finally, a bomb exploded on September 16, 1920, in New York's Wall Street financial district, the very heart of America's capitalist system, and claimed thirty-eight lives. When these terrorist attacks were traced to foreign-born anarchists operating in the United States, public suspicions deepened about *all* left-wing reformers and organizations, even though most of them had also been horrified by the attacks. During this time, in fact, anyone who expressed doubts about the war or nonconformist ideas about American culture or politics ran the risk of being ostracized within his or her community.

Public anger with "radicals" and "troublemakers" soared even higher when the labor movement carried out disruptive work stoppages across the country in 1919 and 1920. These strike actions included a police strike in Boston, a steel strike in Pittsburgh, and a "general strike" (a coordinated strike across multiple industries) in Seattle. All of these strikes had been called by unions determined to secure better wages, which had not kept pace with the price of food, clothing, and other essentials during the war. But they all failed, in large part because business owners, pro-management politicians, and conservative newspapers convinced the public that the strikers were unpatriotic "Reds," a term for Communists that quickly came into common usage. Pointing out that many union members were either the sons of immigrants or immigrants themselves, labor's opponents insinuated that the strikers were wild-eyed foreign radicals who wanted to destroy the American way of life.

The Lusk Committee and the Palmer Raids

Frightened by the swirl of speculation about freedom-hating radicals and Communist sympathizers in their midst, many Americans demanded action from their government. State and federal officials rushed to respond. The New York State Legislature created one of the best-known anti-Communist organizations of this era, the Joint Legislative Committee to Investigate Seditious Activities. Chaired by Senator Clayton Lusk, it quickly became known as the Lusk Committee. For more than a year, Lusk oversaw a wide-ranging investigation to identify, arrest, and prosecute Communists, Socialists, IWW members, and other radicals operating in the state of New York. During the course of its investigation, the Lusk Committee ordered raids on dozens of offices, schools, and homes that it identified as gathering places for radicals. These raids resulted in thousands of arrests and the seizure of huge numbers of documents.

Positive public response to the committee's work also contributed to the New York State Assembly's January 1920 decision to expel five Socialist members—despite the fact that all five had been fairly elected to office. This expulsion outraged many Americans, who saw it as a frightening sign of political repression and disregard for constitutional rights. The victims of this ouster, meanwhile, warned that the majority's attempts to stamp out peaceful political dissent could backfire some day. "We refuse to go to the battlefield until we have fought it out at the ballot box," Charles Solomon, one of the targeted assemblymen, told the legislature. "But if we ever do go to the bayonet the blame will be on your head."[4]

With the exception of its influence over events in the New York State Assembly, though, the Lusk Committee's much-publicized investigation did not amount to much in the end. The committee's final report contained little evidence that any of the targeted groups had been engaged in illegal activity. As a result, only a handful of the more than 1,000 people arrested in the raids were ever deported or convicted of criminal charges.

A far more explosive impact was made by the U.S. Justice Department, which conducted a massive crackdown against radical political groups in

Attorney General A. Mitchell Palmer led the so-called Palmer Raids against "subversives" in America in 1919-1920.

America in 1919-1920 under Attorney General A. Mitchell Palmer. When Palmer, nicknamed the "Fighting Quaker," first became attorney general in March 1919, he resisted the growing public hysteria about Bolshevik plotters in America's midst. One of his first acts as attorney general was to release 10,000 aliens of German ancestry who had been taken into custody during World War I, when the United States was at war with Germany. He also criticized organizations of private citizens like the American Protective League (APL). These self-proclaimed "patriot" groups had become notorious for harassing German immigrants and other ethnic groups they suspected of disloyalty.

As time passed, however, events changed Palmer's perspective. The attorney general was targeted in both of the anarchists' bombing campaigns of 1919, and in the second of these attacks he and his family were nearly killed by a bomb planted on the porch of his home. Palmer remained calm in the face of this close call, but the bombings increased political pressure on him to bring the full weight of his department down on "radical aliens."

The mounting criticism affected Palmer, who harbored dreams of running for president one day. In the summer of 1919 he ordered the Justice Department's Bureau of Investigation (which later became the Federal Bureau of Investigation or FBI) to launch an investigation into radical groups and individuals. Within a matter of months this investigation, which was headed by a young agent named J. Edgar Hoover, had compiled files on tens of thousands of people—both American citizens and alien immigrants—living in the United States.

Some of the people targeted by Hoover for surveillance and other types of investigation were ordinary labor organizers or progressive reformers who had no interest in toppling America's economic or political systems. Other subjects appeared to be chosen for political reasons, such as Assistant Secretary of Labor Louis F. Post, a well-known champion of immigrant rights. Most, however, were members of different Communist parties that had been founded in America in late 1919 by radical Socialist activists who had become attracted to Communism. These groups *did* openly call for armed insurrection against the U.S. government. In 1921 these distinct parties merged into a single Communist Party of America—later known as the Communist Party USA—under direct orders from Moscow's Comintern.

Palmer used the information gathered by Hoover's task force to conduct a series of major raids on suspected radicals. The first of what came to be known as the Palmer Raids took place on November 7, 1919, in twelve American cities. Hundreds of suspected Communists were arrested, and nearly 200 of them were ultimately deported to Russia because of their political beliefs. The initial response to the Palmer Raids was extremely favorable, although a few people argued that deportation was not a harsh enough punishment for those who had been arrested. "If I had my way," declared Massachusetts secretary of the commonwealth Albert Langtry, "I'd take them out in the yard every morning and shoot them, and the next day would have a trial to see whether they were guilty."[5] Encouraged by the positive public reaction, Palmer approved a second series of raids, which were carried out by Hoover in early January 1920. These raids were even more ambitious, extending into thirty cities and towns and snaring between 3,000 and 5,000 people.

Controversy over the Palmer Raids

Many Americans applauded the second round of Palmer Raids, but a growing number of citizens expressed doubts about the crackdown. They argued that the Justice Department was showing little concern about protecting the constitutional rights of the people being targeted. The treatment of those arrested also sparked criticism, as many were held in custody for months in filthy jail cells, subjected to beatings, and denied access to lawyers or family. In many cases arrested individuals endured all of this ill-treatment, only to be released without ever being charged with a crime.[6]

In addition, concerned lawyers, public officials, and journalists warned that the Palmer Raids—combined with the nearly simultaneous decision by the New York Assembly to kick out duly elected representatives because of

The First Amendment and Freedom of Speech

During both the Red Scare and the later McCarthy era, the United States passed laws that trampled on the First Amendment of the Constitution. This amendment was created by America's Founding Fathers for the express purpose of protecting Americans holding unpopular political and religious views from prosecution or harassment. They believed that if people holding minority views were subject to such treatment, then America would become a land of majority tyranny rather than a land of freedom and liberty. The First Amendment reads: "Congress must not interfere with freedom of religion, speech or press, assembly, and petition. Congress shall make no law respecting an establishment of religion, or prohibiting the free exercise thereof; or abridging the freedom of speech, or of the press; or the right of the people peaceably to assemble, and to petition the government for a redress of grievances."

their Socialist political beliefs—showed that the United States was developing a frightening lack of regard for minority rights, which had always been an important element of America's political system. As one newspaper editorial said, "Shall we sometime see Republicans excluding Democrats and Democrats excluding Republicans from our lawmaking bodies, on the ground that the other party's principles are 'inimical to the best interests' of the United States?"[7] U.S. attorney for the Eastern District of Pennsylvania Francis Fisher Kane was so disgusted by the Palmer Raids that he resigned in protest. "It seems to me that the policy of raids against large numbers of individuals is generally unwise and very apt to result in injustice," he wrote in his resignation letter to Palmer and President Woodrow Wilson. "People not really guilty are likely to be arrested and railroaded through their hearings.... We appear to be attempting to repress a political party."[8]

Supporters of the raids and the New York Assembly's actions rushed forward in defense. The *Washington Post* spoke for millions of Americans when it asserted that "there is no time to waste on hairsplitting over infringements of liberty."[9] Palmer himself defended the raids and the overall performance of his Justice Department in congressional testimony. "I am firmly convinced our people want to send back to his own country the plotters who seeks to transplant the chaos of unhappy Russia upon our shores. I am equally convinced that our people want to mete out severe punishment to the citizen, native or naturalized, who joins forces with the alien anarchist in his wicked attempts to injure the Government whose policy of protection of the weak and oppressed makes his presence here possible."[10]

As the debate over the Palmer Raids raged, though, the prospect of similar raids dimmed. In June 1920 Massachusetts judge George Anderson ordered the release of a number of aliens arrested in the Justice Department sweeps. He ruled that agents had engaged in all sorts of illegal activity in their zeal to snare suspected radicals. "A mob is a mob," declared the judge, "whether made up of Government officials acting under instructions from the Department of Justice, or of criminals and loafers and the vicious classes."[11] Anderson's ruling was a big blow to Palmer, whose tenure as attorney general ended less than a year later with the close of the Wilson administration.

Red-Baiting and the Politics of the 1920s

Even with the end of the Palmer Raids, though, the political and social environment in the United States that existed in the 1920s was far different than the one that had been in place a decade earlier. Labor unions that had been enjoying steady growth in membership and power now lay in ruins. Teachers in some school districts had to sign "loyalty oaths" before they could go into the classroom. Far-left political groups that had been an energetic and noisy part of America's political scene virtually disappeared, with some dissolving and others going underground to avoid persecution. Immigration to America from Russia, Italy, Poland, and other countries where Communism and socialism were influential was severely curtailed with passage of the Immigration Act of 1924. And many Americans who had once proudly described themselves as progressives stopped doing so out of a fear that their friends and neighbors would accuse them of being disloyal Reds.

This fear was not a far-fetched one. To the contrary, conservative American politicians, newspaper publishers, and business owners learned during the 1920s that branding liberal opponents as Bolsheviks, Communists, or Reds could be a very effective political weapon. This strategy was used by a wide range of conservative groups, from people who blamed growing efforts to teach evolution in schools on "Communists from New York City"[12] to the American Medical Association (AMA), which described campaigns to control skyrocketing health care costs through government health insurance programs as "socialism and communism—inciting to revolution."[13]

In the meantime, the Justice Department and its various agencies, including Hoover's Bureau of Investigation, relentlessly warned that Americans needed to remain vigilant against possible Communist agents in their midst. These warnings were partially based on a genuine conviction that the threat from Reds remained real, despite the greatly weakened state of the American Communist Party (by the close of the 1920s it could claim only about 7,000 members, most of them centered in and around New York City). But the dark warnings also benefited the Bureau of Investigation and other law enforcement agencies, because as long as Americans remained fearful of Reds, Congress was willing to shovel larger and larger amounts of money into the operations of these agencies. During the 1920s, it became clear to Hoover and other law enforcement officials that the more frightened Americans were about Communists, the more power and prestige they would be able to gather for themselves and their agencies.

American Communism Makes Gains

By the late 1920s Communism in America looked to be on the brink of extinction. Demoralized and fearful, the few Americans who believed in the Communist political system were almost completely isolated from the society in which they lived. Ironically, this isolation was further intensified by the Comintern, which in 1928 had ordered the Communist Party of America not to associate with any other left-wing political organizations. According to the Comintern, even the Socialists were too "impure" for their taste.

But then the Great Depression swept across the United States and the world, and the fortunes of the American Communists began to change. This shattering economic downturn began in October 1929 with a spectacular stock market crash that exposed serious problems with banking systems in the United States and around the world. Many businesses, from family-owned shops to big corporations, were driven to bankruptcy, and unemployment spiked to levels never before seen in the United States. Homelessness, hunger, and other byproducts of abject poverty soared as well. By 1933, when Democrat Franklin D. Roosevelt was elected to the presidency on the promise of delivering a New Deal to increasingly desperate working-class families, public confidence in America's capitalist economic system had been shaken to its core.

As concerns about Communism mounted in the 1920s, the power and influence of J. Edgar Hoover (seen here in 1924) and the Bureau of Investigation increased steadily.

The Depression gave the Communists the opportunity they needed to attract new members. Their campaign to gain new recruits from the ranks of America's disillusioned, out-of-work men and women sputtered at first. In 1932, for example, Communist presidential candidate William Zebulon Foster received only 103,000 votes. Socialist candidate Norman Thomas, meanwhile, tallied seven times that amount, and Roosevelt garnered nearly twenty-three million votes.

But as the Depression continued on, month after month, the Communist message of a classless society in which no one was rich *or* poor began to resonate with some desperate Americans. In addition, some Americans were attracted to Communism's strong support for the labor movement and racial equality. Meanwhile, the American Communist Party benefited from events

19

Communists march in a May Day Parade in Detroit, Michigan, in 1932.

overseas. The rising power of Fascist dictators Adolf Hitler in Germany and Benito Mussolini in Italy gave birth to a new fear in American living rooms. Growing numbers of Americans began to argue that Fascism—a far right-wing belief in the supremacy of the military state and a corresponding contempt for individual rights—posed a greater threat to the United States than Communism. American Communists seized on this development, taking every opportunity to portray Communism as the mortal enemy of Fascism.

The Communist cause also benefited from a wave of favorable media coverage in the early 1930s. Influential magazines like *Harper's*, *Atlantic Monthly*, and *Scribner's* all published major articles that urged readers to try to understand—rather than simply fear—the people and politics of the Soviet Union.[14]

Thousands of curious Americans visited the Soviet Union during this time as well, and many returned home issuing reports of a fast-growing country that respected its workers. These travelers "brought back, shimmering like a mirage, the image of the perfect society," wrote one scholar. "Stirred by the heroism and sacrifices it took to create a new system, they praised its humane system of fraternity. Others had made up their minds before reaching Moscow, and looked only for evidence that would support their convictions."[15]

In addition, American Communists benefited greatly from the Comintern's decision in August 1935 to end its isolation from other left-wing groups. The Comintern instead determined that Communists should join forces with Socialists and other movements of the left in a "popular front" against Fascism. This shift enabled Communists to join up with Socialists, labor unions, and other "champions of the American worker."

By the late 1930s Communists and other activists who were at least sympathetic to some principles of Communism had moved into positions of significant power in a variety of left-wing organizations. They made especially significant progress in labor unions, which had experienced tremendous growth thanks to Roosevelt's pro-labor New Deal policies. Communists were benefited in this area by the mid-1930s emergence of a major new labor organization known as the Congress of Industrial Organizations (CIO). The CIO had been formed by industrial labor leaders who left the conservative American Federation of Labor (AFL) over disagreements about strategy and philosophy. CIO leaders were so eager to unionize steel, automobile, and other industries that they welcomed anyone—including Communists—with organizing experience. As a result, Communist party members were able to move into a number of local, regional, and even national leadership positions within CIO unions. "The Communists made great strides" during this period, summarized historian David Oshinsky. "They joined new organizations, penetrated old ones, and created many of their own—the Communist fronts. Bearing humanitarian titles like the American League for Peace and Democracy, these fronts appealed to people who admired the Soviet achievement or feared the rise of Fascism, but who were left cold by the rigidity of [Communist] Party life. Some who joined may have been unaware of the Communist presence; others simply accepted the Communists as partners—and leaders—in the fight for a 'safer world.'"[16]

Finally, Communists and Communist "sympathizers" entered the federal government during the 1930s and early 1940s, though historians hotly debate whether they numbered in the dozens or the hundreds. Some of these men and women were secret Soviet spies who tried to erase all evidence of their ties to the Communists. But others were not so careful about disguising their past or present associations with Reds. Many of them had long rejected Communism, and they passed off their previous exploration of the system as little more than youthful curiosity. Others did not worry about hiding their past ties because being called a Red did not seem like such a big deal anymore, or because political freedom seemed like something the country valued again. And still others quietly subscribed to political beliefs that had Communist or Socialist elements, but did not engage in any sabotage or spying activity. Instead, they merely advocated for those beliefs in the agencies for which they worked. But as the 1930s drew to a close, all of these different people—as well as Americans who had no association with Reds whatsoever—became the focus of a sustained and fearsome government campaign of "Commie hunting" that roiled the nation.

Notes

[1] Higham, John. *Strangers in the Land: Patterns of American Nativism, 1860-1925.* Rev. ed. Piscataway, NJ: Rutgers University Press, 2002, p. 4.

[2] Oshinsky, David M. *A Conspiracy So Immense: The World of Joe McCarthy.* New York: Free Press, 1983, p. 86.

[3] Roche, John P. *The Quest for the Dream.* New York: Macmillan, 1963.

[4] Quoted in Gage, Beverly. *The Day Wall Street Exploded: A Story of America in Its First Age of Terror.* New York: Oxford University Press, p. 195.

[5] Quoted in Oshinsky, p. 87.

[6] Ackerman, Kenneth D. *Young J. Edgar: Hoover, the Red Scare, and the Assault on Civil Liberties.* Cambridge, MA: Da Capo Press, 2008, p. 6.

[7] Quoted in Murray, Robert K. *Red Scare: A Study in National Hysteria, 1919-1920.* St. Paul: University of Minnesota, 1955, pp. 242-43.

[8] Quoted in Coben, Stanley. *A. Mitchell Palmer: Politician.* New York: Columbia University Press, 1963, p. 230.

[9] "The Red Assassins," *Washington Post,* January 4, 1920.

[10] Palmer, A. Mitchell. Testimony on Charges Made Against Department of Justice by Louis F. Post and Others. Hearings before the Committee on Rules, House of Representatives, 66th Congress, 2nd session, 1920.

[11] Quoted in Post, Louis F. *The Deportations Delirium of Nineteen-twenty: A Personal Narrative of an Historic Official Experience.* New York: Charles H. Kerr, 1923, p. 97.

[12] Oshinsky, p. 89.

[13] *Journal of the American Medical Association-JAMA,* 99, no. 23, December 1932, pp. 1950-1952.

[14] Lowenstein, Meno. *American Opinion of Soviet Russia.* Washington, DC: American Council on Public Affairs, 1941, pp. 129-32.

[15] Morgan, Ted. *Reds: McCarthyism in Twentieth-Century America.* New York: Random House, 2003, p. 166.

[16] Oshinsky, p. 91.

Chapter Two

HUAC AND THE EARLY COLD WAR

Never forget the fact that Communists operating in our midst are in effect a secret battalion of spies and saboteurs parachuted by a foreign foe inside our lines at night and operating as American citizens under a variety of disguises.

—American Legion national commander James F. O'Neil, "How You Can Fight Communism," 1948

The late 1930s and 1940s marked an ominous new chapter in America's efforts to stamp out Communist political activity and espionage. During the 1930s thousands of American citizens had joined Communist groups or lent their talents to Communist political and social causes. In most cases, they had done so out of a genuine interest in making the world a better place, not out of a desire to topple the United States. But the labor movement's growing power, World War II, and the Cold War dramatically increased public suspicion of Americans with any history of involvement in Red organizations or causes. So when investigative groups such as the House Un-American Activities Committee (HUAC) began prowling the countryside looking for Soviet spies and saboteurs, the general public raised little objection—even after it became clear that the political freedoms and legal rights of those targeted for investigation were being pushed aside. Some of the investigations, such as the famous one that targeted State Department official Alger Hiss, ultimately uncovered evidence that Soviet spies were in fact operating in America. But other Americans who were never engaged in espionage also lost their jobs and reputations in the nation's relentless hunt for Communists.

The Dies Committee

The government's investigation of the Red threat was led during the late 1930s and 1940s by a special committee founded in 1938 in the U.S. House of Representatives. HUAC was created in response to escalating conservative anxiety during the mid-1930s about Communist infiltration of labor unions and the "radical" nature of President Franklin D. Roosevelt's New Deal policies. According to military veterans belonging to the American Legion, small businessmen of the Chamber of Commerce, leaders of the conservative American Federation of Labor (AFL), media personalities such as the anti-Semitic Father Charles Coughlin, and other right-wing elements of American society, Communists were acquiring frightening levels of power in the labor movement and the federal government.

In 1936 Roosevelt had tried to blunt these politically damaging charges by giving the Federal Bureau of Investigation (FBI) greater authority to investigate political extremists on both the left and right. This shift in policy delighted FBI director J. Edgar Hoover, a fierce foe of Communism who had first made his mark in law enforcement as a pursuer of Reds. But it was not enough to satisfy conservative lawmakers in Washington. An alliance of Republicans and conservative southern Democrats hostile to Roosevelt's liberal reform policies thus approved the creation of HUAC, a congressional committee specifically dedicated to rooting out Communists (and Nazis, to a lesser degree) in American government and society.

When HUAC began in 1938 it was headed by Texas Democrat Martin Dies, a racist legislator who was contemptuous of Roosevelt and his New Deal policies. But Dies was not the only committee member who felt this way. To the contrary, a majority of HUAC's members were Republicans or southern Democrats deeply opposed to the New Deal. Dies thus had free rein to use his powers as chairman to hammer the Roosevelt administration at every turn. Observers in Washington quickly recognized that with HUAC, America's conservative political movement had gained a valuable new weapon. Roosevelt's vice president, "Cactus" Jack Garner, even went so far as to predict that "the Dies Committee is going to have more influence on the future of American politics than any other committee of congress."[1]

Dies and HUAC attacked Roosevelt in a variety of ways. For example, they frequently insinuated—or outright proclaimed—that New Deal programs were inspired by Communist ideas or led by men and women who

According to some conservative critics, the liberal New Deal policies of President Franklin D. Roosevelt created a pro-Communist environment in Washington.

were either disciples of Communism or easily manipulated by officials who were Reds. Dies personally called for the resignation or dismissal of several leading New Deal reformers, including interior secretary Harold Ickes and labor secretary Frances Perkins. He even called First Lady Eleanor Roosevelt "one of the most valuable assets … the Communist Party possesses."[2]

But HUAC's main strategy for hurting the Roosevelt White House was to publicize "findings" indicating that Communism in America was on the rise under his watch. Dies made particularly effective use of testimony from disillusioned former Communists, who described the movement as a dire threat to American security. Their testimony gave the committee the political cover it needed to expand its investigations without fear of reprisals. Within weeks of conducting its first hearings, HUAC rolled out a list of 640 organizations, 438 newspapers, and 280 labor groups that were possible Communist fronts. Among these names were organizations that *did* have a significant Communist presence, and even historians that are very critical of the Dies Committee admit that it did uncover the identities of some Communist agents and sympathizers who posed a potential threat to national security. But the list also included civil rights groups like the American Civil Liberties Union (ACLU), which had criticized Red-hunting campaigns for abusing individual civil liberties. It even accused popular mainstream organizations like the Boy Scouts and the Campfire Girls, which had committed the offense of encouraging greater understanding between nations, of engaging in "subversive" behavior.

By the end of 1938 the Dies Committee, as it came to be known, had publicly charged more than 1,120 government workers of either being "card-carrying" Reds or sympathetic to Communist ideology. "Martin Dies named more names in one single year than Joe McCarthy named in a life time," marveled historian Robert Griffith.[3] But when accused workers demanded to see the evidence against them, Dies frequently refused to comply. He stated that he was not "at liberty" to provide the incriminating information. HUAC targets were thus left without any means of restoring or defending their reputations. Meanwhile, Americans from all walks of life were hauled before the committee and subjected to hours of grueling questioning. Many Americans called to testify were selected solely because their names appeared on a mailing list belonging to an organization under known or suspected Communist influence.

None of these developments troubled supporters of the Dies Committee, which included many of the country's leading newspapers. Powerful newspaper chains owned by conservative publishers William Randolph Hearst and Robert R. McCormick regularly trumpeted the patriotism of Dies and his HUAC allies. This support remained steadfast throughout the three years that the Dies Committee convened. Meanwhile, these same newspapers ignored or ridiculed HUAC critics who asserted that the Dies Committee was purposely using subpoenas, contempt citations, and other legal powers to intimidate witnesses and ruin the lives and reputations of people it disliked.

As the work of the Dies Committee continued, it became increasingly skilled at manipulating the press and large sectors of the American public into believing that any individual that it placed under investigation was automatically guilty. Federal employees, labor organizers, and ordinary Americans with liberal political beliefs thus came to live in constant fear that they might become the next HUAC target. They knew that such a charge could lead to unemployment, severed friendships, and deep emotional pain for their families, who might suddenly find themselves ostracized from the communities in which they lived.

The Hatch Act and the Smith Act

By 1939 Dies had become a national celebrity, and very few politicians of either party were willing to publicly question his committee's methods or findings. When he introduced a resolution in Congress that year for the committee to continue its work, the House voted 344 to 45 in favor of the resolution, which also boosted its funding. (HUAC was initially formed as a "select" or temporary committee, so it needed annual approval from Congress to continue until 1945, when it was made a "standing" or permanent committee of the House.)

The Dies Committee's success in heightening public fears about Communism was reflected in other ways as well. In 1939 the United States passed a law—the Hatch Act—which made loyalty to the United States a condition for federal employment. In addition, the act greatly restricted the political activities of federal employees, a measure designed to prevent managers from pressuring employees to engage in

During his tenure as head of the House Un-American Activities Committee (HUAC), Representative Martin Dies became Washington's best-known anti-Communist crusader.

activities against (or on behalf of) particular political candidates or parties. The Hatch Act led U.S. attorney general Francis Biddle to carry out secret "loyalty" screenings of federal employees from 1940 to 1943. This exercise also resulted in the creation of the first Attorney General's List of Subversive Organizations (AGLOSO).[4] Several years later, AGLOSOs would become a prominent part of efforts to ferret out Reds lurking in the U.S. government.

In 1940 Congress passed the Alien Registration Act. This law, better known as the Smith Act, was crafted to cripple the Communist Party USA and the German-American Bund, an American Nazi organization founded in the 1930s under the instructions of Adolf Hitler (see "The Smith Act Takes

Aim at American Communists," p. 135). The Smith Act made it illegal for any Americans to "knowingly or willfully advocate, abet, advise, or teach the duty, necessity, desirability or propriety of overthrowing or destroying any government in the United States by force or violence." Many liberal Americans criticized the law, claiming that it put unconstitutional restrictions on free speech. But Roosevelt quietly supported the legislation, and it passed the Senate by voice vote and the House by a lopsided 392-4 margin.

American-Soviet Relations during World War II

High public support for these laws was due in part to the fears of "Commie" infiltration stirred up by the Dies Committee. Another major factor, however, was a nonaggression pact that Soviet leader Joseph Stalin signed with Hitler in the summer of 1939. News of a treaty between the world's most powerful Communist and Fascist nations outraged and frightened the American public. Their fears became even more pronounced in subsequent weeks, when Soviet troops invaded sections of Poland, Finland, Romania, Estonia, Latvia, and Lithuania.

These early World War II events had a huge impact on American Communists, who were already reeling from the anti-Communist crusades of Dies and his many allies. Over the previous few years, their main defense had been to remind people that the Communist leadership of the Soviet Union had adopted a firmer stance against Nazi Germany's expansionist goals than any other nation, including the United States. With the signing of the treaty, though, even that defense had vanished. Liberal and conservative Americans alike blasted the Communists as treacherous snakes. Arrests of Communists by the FBI and local police agencies jumped to levels not seen since the Palmer Raids of 1919-1920.

By early 1941 it appeared that organized Communism in America was on the verge of extinction. Membership in Communist organizations—which had never been very high—plummeted to new lows as fears about legal prosecution and disillusionment about the Soviet-German pact took their toll. On June 22, 1941, however, Hitler's forces invaded the Soviet Union, which responded by throwing the full weight of its huge Red Army against the Nazis. Less than six months later, Germany's World War II ally Japan bombed the U.S. naval base at Pearl Harbor in Hawaii. The unprovoked attack brought the United States into World War II against the so-called Axis Powers of Germany, Japan, and Italy—and on the side of the Soviet Union.

The United States and Russia fought on the same side in World War II, resulting in a temporary easing of Red fears. This photograph was taken at a 1943 war conference attended by Soviet leader Joseph Stalin (left), U.S. president Franklin D. Roosevelt (center), and British prime minister Winston Churchill (right).

This sudden turn of events triggered an amazing shift in American opinion about the Russians. A few months earlier, they were widely vilified as evil practitioners of a corrupt and heartless political philosophy. But after the United States and the Soviet Union became wartime allies, American newspapers and radio programs described the Communists in Russia as valiant and steadfast. The American public remained distrustful of the Communists, but reports of heavy Russian losses blunted much of their traditional hostility. Even HUAC's influence subsided during the war years. As historian Albert Fried wrote, "Who [could] not admire the Soviet Union, America's comrade-in-arms, for its heroism, for the incalculable suffering it endured, in throwing back the monstrous evil of Nazism?"[5]

American policies toward the Soviet Union also underwent a sudden change. Between 1941 and 1946 the United States sent to the Soviets more than $11 billion in military planes, ships, tanks, and other supplies via a "lend-lease" program. The Roosevelt administration also provided some scientific and engineering knowledge to the Soviet military to aid its efforts against German forces. All told, the U.S. government permitted an estimated 15,000 Soviet engineers, technicians, analysts, and scientists to tour American factories and military installations so that they could gather information to improve their own operations.[6]

The Cold War Stokes Renewed Red Fears

The improved relations between the United States and the Soviet Union, however, crumbled when the war came to a close. Shortly after the conflict ended in the spring of 1945 with an Allied victory, the Soviet Union installed Communist governments across a wide swath of eastern Europe, much of which had been occupied by the Red Army during the war's final months. Within a year, influential U.S. foreign policy experts were warning that the Soviets' ultimate goal was worldwide domination. Or as former British prime minister Winston Churchill put it in his famous "Iron Curtain" speech of March 1946, "Soviet Russia and its communist international organization [have set their sights on] the indefinite expansion of their power and doctrines."[7]

As relations between the United States and the Soviet Union deteriorated, public fears about Red agents undermining America from within bubbled to the surface once again. In many cases, these anxieties were stoked by public officials. In late 1945, for example, FBI director J. Edgar Hoover declared that "it behooves us to be on guard for an enemy that brazenly and openly has advocated the corruption of America, that spends sleepless nights working one propaganda line after another, that poses behind a dozen fronts, that squirms and twists his way into those great American forces such as the church, schools, and the ranks of labor."[8] A few years later, U.S. attorney general J. Howard McGrath bluntly asserted that "there are today many Communists in America. They are everywhere—in factories, offices, butcher shops, on street corners, in private businesses—and each carries with him the germs of death for society."[9] Similar bleak pronouncements were issued by a host of senators, diplomats, foreign policy experts, newspaper columnists, and ministers across the country.

By late 1945 the Communist threat had become a huge political issue. Day after day, the Republican Party hammered President Harry S. Truman, a Democrat who had succeeded Roosevelt upon his death on April 12, 1945, for being "soft on communism." With one eye on the fast-approaching 1946 elections, Republicans alleged that under Roosevelt and Truman all levels of federal government had been thoroughly infiltrated by Reds and "Pinkos"—Socialists and others who were sympathetic to Communism even if they were not actual Communist Party members. House Republican leader Joe Martin pledged that if Republicans gained control of Congress, their highest priority would be to "[clean] out the Communists, their fellow travelers and parlor pinks from high positions in our Government."[10]

Harry Truman, seen here making his first address as U.S. president, was repeatedly accused by Republican political opponents of being "soft on communism."

The Republicans' "Red-baiting" strategy helped them win control of both the Senate and the House in the November 1946 elections. These victories gave Republicans control of Congress for the first time since 1933. They also brought a wave of relatively unknown lawmakers to Washington. Before long, however, two of those politicians—Republican senator Joseph McCarthy of Wisconsin and Republican representative Richard Nixon of California—would rank among the nation's most famous anti-Communist crusaders.

Truman Orders Loyalty Reviews

Two weeks after the November 1946 election results came in, Truman announced the creation of the President's Temporary Commission on Employee Loyalty (TCEL). This committee was charged with reviewing all of the federal government's loyalty programs and establishing procedures to remove or disqualify "any disloyal or subversive person" from federal service. Truman's support for the TCEL was not based on any deep conviction that the federal government was riddled with Communist agents. To the contrary, Truman remarked privately in early 1947 that "people are very much wrought up about the Communist 'bugaboo' but I am of the opinion that the country is perfectly safe so far as Communism is concerned."[11] The creation of the TCEL, then, stemmed mostly from Truman's belief that he needed to blunt the political impact of the Republicans' "soft on communism" charges.

> *U.S. attorney general J. Howard McGrath asserted that "there are today many Communists in America. They are everywhere—in factories, offices, butcher shops, on street corners, in private businesses—and each carries with him the germs of death for society."*

Truman's confidence about America's internal security, though, did not mean that he was unconcerned about the Soviet Union's actions and goals. Truman believed that Stalin's empire posed a genuine risk to world peace. On March 12, 1947, he appeared before a joint session of Congress and unveiled a new foreign policy based on the containment of Communist expansion. This policy, which became known as the Truman Doctrine, reflected the fact that Europe's war losses made the United States the only nation capable of standing up to the Soviets. The Truman Doctrine thus stood as an important event in the early stages of the so-called "Cold War"—the tense rivalry that arose between the United States (and its allies) and the Soviet Union and other Communist countries after World War II.

Nine days after his appearance before Congress, Truman issued Executive Order 9835, which prescribed "procedures for the administration of an employee loyalty program in the executive branch of the federal government." This executive order, which was based on the findings of the TCEL, established a loyalty program *requiring* that all existing and prospective federal employees be screened to ensure that they were "loyal" Americans. Under this program, anyone found to have even the most remote association with subversive groups could be barred from employment. The list of suspicious groups would be compiled and maintained in a new Attorney General's List of Subversive Organizations (AGLOSO).

The practical impact of the Truman administration's decision to make Communism illegal was to transform "party members from political dissidents into criminals—with all the implications that such associations inspired in a nation of law-abiding citizens."[12] Yet few Americans voiced objections to Truman's creation of a government program that punished people for associations with unpopular political organizations. Most of the organizations and newspapers that issued protests did not focus on whether the program violated the basic constitutional rights of citizens. Instead, they argued that groups whose names appeared on the AGLOSO deserved an opportunity to defend themselves before they were listed, that clear standards should be established for "subversive" status, and that the listing should be published so that present and prospective federal employees knew which organizational affiliations were potentially dangerous to their careers.[13] These arguments convinced the Truman administration to make the AGLOSO list public in December 1947 rather than keep it secret, as the government had done in the early 1940s. Many Americans were relieved by the decision because it enabled them to avoid the organizations that might cost them their jobs and reputations.

Red Hysteria—or a Genuine Threat?

Some Americans resisted the rising tide of fear and paranoia about Communism in America. They recognized that some of the warnings of Communist infiltration were based on hysteria rather than fact, and that other charges were politically motivated. This resistance to Red-baiting was especially strong among educated and progressive-minded individuals and organizations that rejected conservative efforts to equate all liberal or humanitarian political beliefs with Communism. The biggest fear of these Americans was that paranoia about Communist agents was driving state-sponsored destruction of the nation's constitutional foundations, such as freedom of speech and freedom of political association.

In the late 1940s, however, their voices were drowned out by a series of events that further increased public anxiety about Communism in America. One such event was organized labor's decision to carry out a major purge of Communists from its ranks. This included the expulsion of all known Communists from the United Auto Workers (UAW) and the 1950 decision by the Congress of Industrial Organizations (CIO) to kick out unions that were determined to be under Communist influence. But the expulsions did not necessarily reassure people that the problem of Communist infiltration of labor had been addressed. Instead, it convinced many Americans that anti-Communist crusaders like Hoover, who had issued dark warnings about labor's links to Communism over the years, were the most trustworthy sources of information.

American anxieties about Communist infiltration were further height-ened by the discovery in the late 1940s of a number of Communist agents who really were secretly carrying out espionage or spying activities in the United States. The existence of many of these agents and spies was revealed to the American people during public hearings carried out by the House Un-American Activities Committee (HUAC). HUAC had faded in influence dur-ing World War II. But it re-emerged as a formidable political force in the late 1940s under the direction of chairman J. Parnell Thomas, a conservative Republican congressman from New Jersey. The Thomas-led HUAC made its first big splash in 1947, when the committee conducted a series of public hearings on the Hollywood film industry. Thomas and other anti-Communist members of the committee said that the hearings were necessary to determine whether film directors, producers, actors, and screenwriters in Hollywood were inserting Communist propaganda into their films.

The Hollywood Ten

The ranks of the vast American film industry did include a scattering of Communists and former Communists. Most of these men and women had begun following Communism during the difficult economic times of the 1930s. But while the 300 or so Communists in Hollywood had become active in the industry's unions, it is unclear whether they had any meaningful influ-ence on the content of the movies on which they worked.[14]

The Hollywood hearings were guaranteed to receive a considerable amount of publicity, given America's great enthusiasm for movies. But they evolved quickly into a full-blown media circus. Famous movie stars like Ronald Reagan and Gary Cooper joined with powerful Hollywood figures such as Walt Disney in claiming that HUAC's suspicions were justified. According to them, Communists had indeed corrupted the American film industry. But whereas individuals like Reagan, who was president of the Screen Actors Guild at the time, gave their testimony willingly, other actors, directors, and writers who were called to testify before HUAC refused to cooperate.

The best-known of these hostile witnesses were a group of writers and directors who argued that HUAC questions about their past or present politi-cal affiliations were blatant violations of their constitutional rights to freedom of speech and association. All of them had been associated with—or members of—Communist organizations at one time or another. But their refusal to tes-

Nine members of the Hollywood Ten in an appearance at the U.S. marshal's office in Los Angeles in December 1947. They are, from left to right: Robert Adrian Scott, Edward Dmytryk, Samuel Ornitz, Lester Cole, Herbert Biberman, Albert Maltz, Alvah Bessie, John Howard Lawson, and Ring Lardner Jr. (the tenth member, Dalton Trumbo, is not in the photo).

tify was also based on the belief that the hearings were essentially a "witch hunt" for Americans with unpopular political views (see "A Communist Screenwriter Defies the House Un-American Activities Committee," p. 139).

The defiance of the Hollywood Ten, as these men came to be known, was supported by many members of the film industry. Famous industry figures such as director John Huston, actor Humphrey Bogart, actress Myrna Loy, and screenwriter Philip Dunne even organized a Committee for the First Amendment to protest the government's treatment of the Hollywood Ten. But

Congress responded angrily to the stance of the Hollywood Ten. All ten were cited for contempt of Congress and sentenced to prison terms of six to twelve months. When the Supreme Court refused to hear their appeal, every one of them went to jail.

The Hollywood Ten episode greatly increased public pressure on the American film industry to prove that it was not riddled with Reds. Panic-stricken studio executives responded in December 1947 with the Waldorf Statement, which denounced the Hollywood Ten and promised to rid Hollywood of all "subversives" (see "Hollywood Studios Issue the 'Waldorf Statement,'" p. 138). Film, television, and radio studios also refused to employ men and women who were thought—rightly or wrongly—to have Communist sympathies or backgrounds. This "blacklisting," as it was called, ruined the careers of hundreds of writers, directors, and actors.

The quick surrender of the studios to the tide of the Red Scare encouraged conservative political activists to press their advantage. This phenomenon was most clearly seen in June 1950, when the publishers of an anti-Communist newsletter released *Red Channels: The Report of Communist Influence in Radio and Television*. This hastily prepared pamphlet included the names of 151 entertainers and writers in Hollywood who, the authors implied, had political associations that should be viewed with suspicion. Some of the men and women listed in *Red Channels* were mainstream liberals who had simply participated in humanitarian or social reform efforts over the years. Others were current or former members of the Communist Party, which was not a criminal offense in and of itself. But this did not matter to the spooked executives in Hollywood. Most of the people listed in *Red Channels* were blacklisted across the movie and broadcast industries for years.

The Case of Alger Hiss

In 1948 HUAC convened another series of public hearings, this time about alleged Communist infiltration of the federal government. In July the committee heard testimony from an American woman named Elizabeth Bentley, who claimed that she had spent several years as a Soviet courier delivering top-secret government documents from Washington officials to Russian agents. Bentley's spectacular story had been known to the FBI and other law enforcement agencies for some time, but they had been unable to secure confessions—or any other evidence of disloyalty—against any of the liberal gov-

A Member of the Hollywood Ten Speaks Out

One of the most prominent members of the Hollywood Ten was Dalton Trumbo, an award-winning screenwriter. Trumbo held Communist beliefs, but he also considered himself to be a loyal American. In 1949, at the height of the controversy surrounding the prosecution of the Hollywood Ten, Trumbo wrote *The Time of the Toad*, in which he urged Americans to recognize that defending people with unpopular political beliefs was integral to the nation's well-being. "The legal principles which protect one against the force of the state protect all," he wrote. "If a Communist comes first under attack and is overwhelmed, the breach opened by his fall becomes an avenue for the advance of the enemy with all his increased prestige upon you. You need not agree with the Communist while you engage in his and your common defense. You may, indeed, oppose him with every honorable weapon in our arsenal.... But defend him you must, for his defeat in the Constitutional battle involves the over-turn of principles which thus far have stood as our principal barrier, short of bloodshed, against fascism."

Source: Trumbo, Dalton. *The Time of the Toad: A Study of Inquisition in America.* New York: Harper and Row, 1972.

ernment officials she had identified as Communist collaborators. Despite the fact that Bentley's story had failed to result in any arrests, however, it electrified the nation when she related it to the committee.

Several of the officials accused of espionage by Bentley were also called to testify at the hearings. All of these men denied the allegations or took the Fifth Amendment (an amendment in the Bill of Rights that states that no citizen may be forced to testify against himself or herself). The frustrated committee then called a *Time* magazine editor and former Communist named Whittaker Chambers to testify. Chambers supported Bentley's story, as expected. But his testimony then went in an unexpected direction, and his remarks unleashed the most famous spy scandal of the entire Cold War era.

During the course of Chambers's testimony, he claimed that several New Deal officials had actually been fellow Communist Party members who

Elizabeth Bentley testifies during an August 11, 1948, appearance before the House Un-American Activities Committee.

engaged in spying activities for the Soviets. The most shocking name given by Chambers was that of Alger Hiss. A highly respected former top State Department official, Hiss had left government work in 1947 to assume the presidency of the Carnegie Endowment for International Peace, a prestigious nonprofit organization dedicated to fostering cooperation between nations.

Hiss promptly volunteered to appear before HUAC. He angrily denied all the charges and declared that he had never met Chambers before. Hiss's denials were so convincing that Truman himself used them to criticize the Republican-led HUAC and its Red-hunting mission. "The public hearings now under way are serving no useful purpose," he said in an August 5 press conference. "On the contrary, they are doing irreparable harm to certain people, seriously impairing the morale of federal employees, and undermining public confidence in the government.... They are slandering a lot of people that don't deserve it."[15]

Unfazed, Chambers repeated his accusations that Hiss was a Communist agent on the radio program *Meet the Press*. Hiss then sued him for libel—making false and malicious public remarks meant to damage a person's reputation. Rather than back down, however, Chambers struck back. Prodded by questioning from HUAC member Richard Nixon, who had emerged as the committee's chief interrogator in the Hiss-Chambers controversy, Chambers provided details about Hiss's personal life that strongly suggested that the two men had once known each other fairly well (see "Whittaker Chambers and Alger Hiss Testify before HUAC," p. 143). He also produced dozens of State Department documents that he alleged had been stolen by Hiss. Most important of all, Chambers led HUAC investigators to a pumpkin patch on his Maryland farm, where he produced a hidden stash of microfilm containing summaries of secret State Department reports. Experts interviewed by HUAC claimed that the summaries had likely been typed on a manual typewriter owned by Hiss.

When a face-to-face meeting arranged by HUAC investigators between Hiss and Chambers failed to elicit a confession from Hiss, the FBI began building a legal case against the former State Department official. On December 15, 1948, a grand jury indicted Hiss on two counts of perjury (the statute of limitations on espionage had run out, so no such charges could be brought against him). Hiss's first trial ended in a hung jury, with eight jurors voting for conviction and four for acquittal. But he was convicted in a second trial in January 1950. Hiss eventually served 44 months in prison. He maintained his innocence for the rest of

Former State Department official Alger Hiss denied that he was a Communist agent when he appeared before the House Un-American Activities Committee, but circumstantial evidence against him was very strong.

his life, and controversy continues to swirl around the case. Most historians, however, now believe that Hiss probably was a Communist at one time—as well as an agent for the Soviets.

The Soviets Acquire "The Bomb"

The high-profile conviction of Hiss gave HUAC and other anti-Communist voices in America more influence than ever. Many Americans viewed his case as convincing proof that the politicians, radio personalities, American Legion members, and newspaper publishers who had been warning about Red infiltration of the State Department and other federal agencies had been right all along. So when other events prompted expressions of outrage or suspicion among influential anti-Communists like Hoover, Thomas, and Nixon—such as growing signs that Communists in China were on the verge of seizing control of that country—the nerves of the American public became even more frayed.

The prospect of "losing" China to Communism struck fear into the hearts of officials and lawmakers all across Washington. But a brief statement issued by the Truman White House on September 23, 1949, caused even greater panic in American living rooms from coast to coast. The statement declared that "we have evidence that within recent weeks an atomic explosion occurred in the USSR." The news that the Soviet Union had now joined America as the only two nations on earth with "The Bomb"—the atomic bomb—struck the United States like a thunderbolt.

The revelation that the Communists now possessed nuclear weaponry also served to feed the mounting hysteria about Red spies in America. Most Americans were convinced that the Russians could not have gained this capability without the theft of U.S. nuclear secrets by undercover agents. Their certainty stemmed partly from the widely held view that the Soviets were both evil and cunning. But it also came from America's idealized view of itself in the years following World War II, when it had played such a pivotal role in the Allied victory. As historian Tom Wicker wrote, post-war Americans believed that they "could do anything, could go anywhere, could stand for any good cause, and were bound inevitably to triumph.... Failure whether in combat or diplomacy could not, therefore, be an American failure, for there was no such thing; failure could only result from subversion, espionage by the evil empire [of the Soviet Union], and treason—betrayal in high places."[16]

Notes

[1] Quoted in Morgan, Ted. *Reds: McCarthyism in Twentieth-Century America.* New York: Random House, 2003, p. 187.

[2] Quoted in Stone, Geoffrey R. *Perilous Times: Free Speech in Wartime from the Sedition Act of 1798 to the War on Terrorism.* New York: W. W. Norton, 2004, p. 246.

[3] Griffith, Robert. *The Politics of Fear: Joseph R. McCarthy and the Senate.* Rev. ed. Amherst: University of Massachusetts Press, 1987, p. 32.

[4] Goldstein, Robert Justin. "Prelude to McCarthyism: The Making of a Blacklist." *Prologue,* Fall 2006, http://www.archives.gov/publications/prologue/2006/fall/agloso.html.

[5] Fried, Albert. *McCarthyism: The Great American Red Scare: A Documentary History.* New York: Oxford University Press, 1996, p. 13.

[6] Overy, Richard. *Why the Allies Won.* New York: W. W. Norton, 1997, p. 253.

[7] Churchill, Winston S. Speech at Westminster College, Fulton, Missouri, March 1946. Reprinted in *Never Give In: The Best of Winston Churchill's Speeches.* New York: Hyperion, 2003.

[8] Hoover, J. Edgar. Speech before the International Association of Police Chiefs, October 28, 1945. U.S. Congress, 79th Congress, 1st session, *Congressional Record,* p. 5410.

[9] Quoted in White, John Kenneth. *Still Seeing Red: How the Cold War Shapes the New American Politics.* Boulder, CO: Westview, 1998, p. 65.

[10] Quoted in Goldstein.

[11] Quoted in Thompson, Francis H. *The Frustration of Politics: Truman, Congress, and the Loyalty Issue, 1945-1953*. Cranbury, NJ: Associated University Press, 1979, p. 27.

[12] Schrecker, Ellen. *The Age of McCarthyism: A Brief History with Documents*. Boston: St. Martin's Press, 1994, p. 21.

[13] Goldstein.

[14] Ceplair, Larry, and Steven Englund. *The Inquisition in Hollywood: Politics in the Film Community, 1930-1960*. Urbana and Chicago: University of Illinois Press, 2003.

[15] Truman, Harry S. Press conference remarks, August 5, 1947. Harry S. Truman Library and Museum, http://www.trumanlibrary.org/publicpapers/index.php?pid=1771.

[16] Wicker, Tom. *Shooting Star: The Brief Arc of Joe McCarthy*. New York: Harcourt, 2006, pp. 15-16.

Chapter Three

THE RISE OF
JOE MCCARTHY

⋙⟡⋘

This is the era of the Armageddon—that final all-out battle
between light and darkness foretold in the Bible.

—Senator Joseph McCarthy

I n the early 1950s one American politician stood out from all of his colleagues in his ability to take advantage of domestic fears about Communism. Senator Joseph McCarthy used American anxiety about Reds to rise
out of obscurity and entrench himself as the single most influential member
of Congress. But his methods, which included wild allegations against thousands of powerless Americans, ruthless manipulation of the media, and
repeated characterizations of political enemies as traitors and cowards, cast a
dark pall over the entire country. By 1953 his crude brand of political warfare
and irresponsible Red-baiting, widely known as McCarthyism, had transformed the United States into a powder keg of fear and suspicion.

Reds in Full Retreat

By the close of the 1940s Communism in the United States had been
almost completely stamped out. Communists no longer had any meaningful
presence in the American labor movement, due to a concerted union effort to
cleanse its ranks of Reds. In addition, the Communist Party USA, which had
never been an important factor in American politics, had withered under the
impact of anti-Communism measures taken by the Truman administration
and internal leadership turmoil. By 1950 the party's membership had
declined to only about 50,000, and many of these members had stopped tak-

ing part in its activities or "gone underground" to avoid legal prosecution. A year later open membership had shrunk to 16,000.[1]

The anti-Communist crusades of the late 1940s had also rooted out the networks of Communist spies that did exist in America. The Alger Hiss case had grabbed the most headlines, but other Soviet agents hidden in the U.S. government had been discovered and prosecuted as well. So when Republican senator Joseph McCarthy of Wisconsin came out of nowhere in 1950 to become the nation's best-known anti-Communist, few legitimate targets still existed for him to investigate. As biographer Tom Wicker wrote, "For all the noise McCarthy made after 1950, he was in fact a latecomer to, and virtually a nonparticipant in, the real anticommunist wars."[2]

World events, though, kept Communist fears at a high level in the United States. Within the space of less than two months in the fall of 1949, Americans learned that the Soviet Union possessed the atomic bomb and that Communist forces had won a long civil war in China, the most highly populated country on the planet. With most of Asia now flying the flag of Communism, Americans expressed rising concern that the Cold War was being lost. This anxiety became a potent political weapon for the Republican Party, which regarded the events in Russia and China as a clear indication that President Truman and the Democrats who controlled Congress did not possess the skill or will to hold back Communism. By early 1950, the Republicans were pounding Truman on a daily basis for "losing" China and allowing the Soviets to build atomic weaponry—possibly with secrets stolen from America's own atomic bomb program. It was in this heated environment that Joe McCarthy delivered one of the most famous political speeches in U.S. history.

America's Newest Political Star

McCarthy was in many ways an unlikely candidate to emerge in 1950 as the nation's leading anti-Communist politician. The Senate included plenty of better-known and more powerful politicians who issued regular warnings about the Red menace, such as Republicans Henry Styles Bridges (New Hampshire), Karl Mundt (South Dakota), and William Jenner (Indiana), and Democrats Pat McCarran (Nevada) and James Eastland (Mississippi). Moreover, McCarthy had fumed about Communist infiltration of the U.S. government ever since his 1946 election to the Senate, with little apparent benefit to his public profile. In 1947, for example, he had compared American Communists "to a huge iceberg in a shipping lane" in a radio interview: "The most

44

Wisconsin senator Joseph McCarthy burst on the national scene in February 1950, when he told a West Virginia audience that he had evidence of Communist agents in the U.S. government.

dangerous part of the iceberg is under water and invisible and you can no more bring the underground communist organizations up to the surface than you can cause that huge iceberg to float upon the face of the sea."[3] He also had a long-running feud with a Wisconsin newspaper, the *Madison Capital Times*, which he accused of being sympathetic to communism.[4]

On February 9, 1950, however, the obscure senator delivered a speech in Wheeling, West Virginia, that made headlines across the United States. McCarthy's Wheeling speech, which was delivered before the local Women's Republican Club, touched on all the standard Republican criticisms that had been leveled against the Roosevelt and Truman administrations over the years. The senator claimed that their post–World War II policies enabled the expansion of Communism overseas, and that their weak response to domestic Communism allowed spies like Alger Hiss to damage national security. None of these charges were new. But McCarthy also claimed in his speech that he had in his personal possession the names of more than 200 Communists *currently* working in Truman's State Department—and that the president and his fellow Democrats actually approved of their presence. In essence,

McCarthy asserted that he had acquired clear evidence that the Democrats were traitors who were actively aiding America's greatest enemy (see "The Speech that Launched McCarthy's Political Rise," p. 152).

McCarthy's dramatic speech, in which he waved around papers that allegedly contained the names of all the State Department Communists, might have faded into the general clamor of anti-Truman rhetoric that was being offered by Republicans at that time. But his appearance was covered by a reporter for the Associated Press (AP), which distributed news stories to newspapers all across the country. When the AP decided to pass along its account of the speech to its clients, many of America's largest newspapers ran the story. Within a matter of hours, McCarthy's alleged evidence of widespread Communist infiltration of the State Department was the most talked-about news story in America.

Reporters from all across the country rushed to McCarthy in hopes that he would give them the 205 names he claimed to possess. Instead, McCarthy changed the number of alleged security risks to 57 and refused to identify them, saying vaguely that he would do so when the time was right. Some journalists were troubled by this development, but most newspapers, radio, and television outlets accepted McCarthy's remarks. Moreover, reporters began congregating around McCarthy wherever he went in hopes that he would deliver another bombshell. The senator was delighted by his sudden emergence into the political spotlight. He still refused to "name names," but he slammed the Truman administration again and again, using fierce language that was guaranteed to keep him in the news. The heavy media coverage allowed the once-unknown senator to become the most famous lawmaker in Congress within a matter of a few months. "The more Americans worried about the Russians, atomic war, loyalty oaths, or spies in government, the more they thought about Joe McCarthy," explained historian David Oshinsky. "And the less certain they seemed about their own future."[5]

New Security Laws Anger Truman

By the summer of 1950 fears of Communist treachery in government had reached a new level of intensity, both in Washington and across the country. McCarthy's inflammatory rhetoric played a large part in this escalating anxiety, even though he failed to produce any evidence to support his accusations. But other factors were also at work, most importantly the June 1950 invasion of South Korea by Communist military forces from North Korea.

Truman promptly sent American troops to South Korea to help repel the invasion, but the U.S. forces suffered a series of military defeats in the opening months of the conflict. The crisis on the Korean Peninsula gave McCarthy and other Republicans further ammunition for their claims that Truman and the Democrats were too weak to ward off the march of Communism.

Responding to the fearful public mood, Congress passed a sweeping security bill into law. The chief sponsors of the Internal Security Act (also known as the Subversive Activities Control Act) were Democratic senator Pat McCarran and Democratic representative John Wood of Georgia, who was chair of the House Un-American Activities Committee. Their bill, which was widely supported by both Republicans and Democrats, legalized the deportation of Communists and other "subversives" from the United States. It also gave the government increased authority to investigate persons suspected of disloyalty, required Communist organizations to register with the U.S. attorney general, and authorized internment camps "for emergency situations."

"The other senators were now afraid to speak their minds, to take issue with [McCarthy]," said Senator Margaret Chase Smith. "It got to the point where some of us refused to be seen with people he disapproved of. A wave of fear had struck Washington."

The McCarran Act, as it was often called, was popular with an American public desperate for reassurance that the Red threat was being addressed. But it became law over the objections of Truman, who tried to kill it with a veto. "In a free country we punish men for the crimes they commit but never for the opinions they have," Truman declared.

> We can and we will prevent espionage, sabotage, or other actions endangering our national security. But we would betray our finest traditions if we attempted, as this bill would attempt, to curb the simple expression of opinion. This we should never do, no matter how distasteful the opinion may be to the vast majority of our people. The course proposed by this bill would delight the communists, for it would make a mockery of the Bill of Rights and of our claims to stand for freedom in the world.... [This act] would open a Pandora's Box of opportunities for official condemnation of organizations and individuals for perfectly honest opinions which happen to be stated also by Communists.[6]

Truman's veto of September 22 did not stand, however. Supporters of the bill easily overrode his veto one day later.

Early Attempts to Stop McCarthy Fail

At the same time that the Internal Security Act was making its way through Congress, McCarthy became the focus of two separate efforts to end his meteoric rise. The first bid came from Democrats on a Senate subcommittee that had been formed in February 1950 to investigate the allegations that McCarthy had made in Wheeling. Formally known as the Subcommittee on the Investigation of Loyalty of State Department Employees, it quickly became known as the Tydings Committee because it was chaired by Millard Tydings, a conservative Democrat from Maryland with a long track record of anti-Communism.

As the investigation wore on, McCarthy told the committee that he knew of 81 State Department employees who were "card-carrying Communists." But State Department officials and journalist Drew Pearson discovered that the only "evidence" McCarthy possessed was an old list of government personnel who had already been investigated—and in many cases cleared—by the FBI. Abandoning his list, McCarthy abruptly accused several other American officials and academics of being Reds. Most notably, the senator called a State Department official named Owen Lattimore "a top Russian spy."[7] But when he failed to substantiate these serious charges, Democrats on the Tydings Committee shifted the target of their investigation to McCarthy and his methods.

On July 17, 1950, the three Democrats on the five-person Tydings Committee released a 300-page final report that declared that McCarthy had perpetrated a "fraud and a hoax ... on the Senate." The report further charged that McCarthy's accusations of massive Communist infiltration of the U.S. government "represent perhaps the most nefarious campaign of half-truths and untruths in the history of this republic." But the two Republicans on the committee refused to support the report, which quickly became the subject of furious debate in the Senate.

Conservative Republicans denounced the Tydings Committee for producing a "Communist whitewash," and McCarthy himself called the report a "clever, evil thing." A number of Senate Republicans claimed that Democrats were trying to destroy a great American, and some, like Senator William Jenner, openly questioned Tydings's own loyalty to his country. The onslaught shocked Tydings, who responded that "you will find out who has been whitewashing—

with mud and slime, with filth, with the dregs of publicity at the expense of the people's love for their country. I ask the Senate: What are you going to do about it? I leave it up to your conscience."[8] In the end, the Democrat-controlled Senate approved the findings of the Tydings Committee, but the vote did not result in any serious consequences for Mc-Carthy. In fact, the whole episode boosted McCarthy's reputation among Republican voters as a gritty fighter.

The other attempt to rein in McCarthy's growing influence was waged by a member of his own party. During the spring of 1950, moderate Republican senator Margaret Chase Smith of Maine had grown alarmed by McCarthy's reckless accusations—as well as the ways in which his irresponsible Red-baiting seemed to be benefit-

On June 1, 1950, Republican senator Margaret Chase Smith of Maine bravely denounced McCarthyism on the floor of the U.S. Senate.

ing him. She also believed that his growing stature in Washington was hurting the American political system. "The other senators were now afraid to speak their minds, to take issue with him," she said. "It got to the point where some of us refused to be seen with people he disapproved of. A wave of fear had struck Washington."[9]

On June 1, 1950, Smith made her concerns public with a speech on the Senate floor. This "Declaration of Conscience," as she called it, was co-sponsored by six other moderate Republicans. A seventh also signed the Declaration after Smith finished her remarks. But it was Smith who composed the speech (with the help of an aide named William Lewis), and it was Smith who delivered it in a strong, clear voice while McCarthy sat only a few rows away (see "Margaret Chase Smith's Declaration of Conscience," p. 158). She did not mention McCarthy by name, but it was clear to everyone in attendance who she was talking about when she declared that the Senate had become "a publicity platform for irresponsible sensationalism." Smith also urged her fellow Republicans to resist Red-baiting in their campaigns for the upcoming elections. "I don't want to see the Republican party ride to victory on the Four Horsemen of Calumny—Fear, Ignorance, Bigotry and Smear."[10]

Many Americans praised Smith for her brave stand, and Truman later told the Republican that her Declaration of Conscience "was one of the finest things that has happened here in Washington in all my years in the Senate and the White House."[11] But most Republicans (and conservative anti-Communist Democrats) declined to endorse her position. Some disagreed with her. Others privately thought she was right, but did not want to reduce McCarthy's usefulness as a political weapon against the Democrats. And some senators remained silent out of fear that McCarthy might turn his talent for character assassination against them. As a result, McCarthy suffered no lasting damage from Smith's speech.

Political Victories Increase McCarthy's Power

With these obstacles behind him, McCarthy became the Republican Party's most popular and effective campaigner for the 1950 midterm elections. He appeared in fifteen states over the next few months to drum up support for Republican congressional candidates. At each stop, he railed against the Truman administration and warned that Democrats were letting Communists run rampant in Washington. Truman responded to these charges with defiance, stating that McCarthy and other Republicans who were embracing the Wisconsin senator's language had lost "all sense of restraint, all sense of patriotic decency."[12] Nonetheless, the Republican strategy paid off, as the party gained twenty-eight seats in the House of Representatives and five seats in the Senate—including the seat that had been held by Tydings, who lost to Republican John Marshall Butler.

Some of this success was due to the fact that the party holding the White House typically loses congressional seats in midterm elections. But many of the victories were credited to McCarthy, who roused many conservative voters to the polls. McCarthy basked in the glow of his newfound status as a political difference-maker, and he expressed particular satisfaction with Butler's victory over Tydings. McCarthy knew that the results in Maryland would make other politicians think twice before they challenged him.

In 1951 McCarthy took his Red-baiting campaign to new depths, issuing repeated condemnations of the country's Democratic leaders. He routinely characterized Truman as soft on Communism, ignoring all kinds of evidence

In the 1950 and 1952 election seasons, McCarthy delivered political speeches all across the country that attacked Democratic officials and candidates as Reds or "Commie sympathizers."

that the president had actually approved and enforced a wide array of anti-Communist measures. Truman had instituted government loyalty programs, overseen a vast expansion in the size of the U.S. military, established American military bases in countries all over the world, and kept U.S. troops in the Korean War even after China joined forces with the North Koreans. In addition, he had approved the creation of the Central Intelligence Agency (CIA), which became the nation's leading spy agency, and helped establish the North American Treaty Organization (NATO), America's chief international military alliance throughout the Cold War era. But none of this mattered to McCarthy or the legions of Americans who accepted his vague, unsubstantiated condemnations as fact.

McCarthy reserved his harshest words for Dean Acheson and George Marshall. The senator condemned Acheson, who served as Truman's secretary of state from 1949 to 1953, as a treasonous ally of the Soviets. In May 1951, for example, McCarthy delivered a speech on the Senate floor in which he used the case of wounded Korean War veteran Bob Smith to launch a vicious attack on Acheson. McCarthy stated that when Bob Smith "gets his artificial limbs," he should walk to the state department office of Acheson and say to him, "Dean, thousands of American boys have faced those twin killers [North Koreans and Chinese] because you and your crimson crowd betrayed us. He should say, 'Mr. Acheson, if you want at long last to perform one service for the American people you should not only resign from the State Department but you should remove yourself from this country and go to the nation [the Soviet Union] for which you have been struggling and fighting so long."[13]

McCarthy Attacks a World War II Hero

One month later, McCarthy delivered an even more shocking speech denouncing General George Marshall, a famous World War II hero who had also served as Truman's secretary of state from 1947 to early 1949. Marshall had not only served his country with distinction in the war, he had been the primary architect of the so-called Marshall Plan. This economic aid program had played an essential role in Europe's post-war recovery and in preventing Fascism or Communist from taking root in many parts of the country. Today, it is almost universally regarded as one of the great American policy triumphs of the twentieth century. But McCarthy criticized the plan, accused Marshall of having Communist leanings, and even insinuated that he could have prevented the Pearl Harbor attack. "How can we account for our present situation unless we believe that men high in this government are concerting to deliver us to disaster?" McCarthy declared in the most infamous passage from his three-hour speech. "This must be the product of a great conspiracy, a conspiracy so immense and an infamy so black as to dwarf any previous such instance in the history of man."[14]

McCarthy's attack triggered a backlash from liberal newspapers and Democrats, but it also angered many conservative Americans who revered Marshall. Military officers and officials from World War II also spoke up, defending Marshall and denouncing McCarthy. "The man who seeks to gain political advantage from personal attack on a secretary of state is a man who seeks to gain political advantage from damage to his country,"[15] grumbled con-

Senator Joseph McCarthy's political power became so great that even Republican president Dwight D. Eisenhower was reluctant to criticize him.

servative Republican Henry L. Stimson, who served as secretary of war during World War II. Within days of the speech, which also angered many of his fellow Republican senators, McCarthy knew that he had miscalculated. From this point on, McCarthy kept Marshall out of the line of his political fire.

McCarthy's verbal assault on Marshall also fed a heated debate among the significant number of Americans who loathed the senator from Wisconsin. Some critics argued that "McCarthyism," as McCarthy's Red-baiting tactics were becoming known, was simply the product of an ambitious and unprincipled politician who had stumbled upon a strategy for increased personal power and prestige. Other detractors asserted that McCarthy was a deeply paranoid man who genuinely believed in the conspiracy theories he was voicing. As time passed, liberal hatred for McCarthy became so all-consuming that on occasions when evidence of Soviet espionage in America *was* uncovered, they too often ignored or downplayed it.

Meanwhile, McCarthy's supporters in the press, the Republican Party, and American neighborhoods insisted that the negative views of the senator were invalid. They continued to praise him as a take-charge legislator who was determined to confront the Red menace wherever it reared its ugly head. And many of his defenders shrugged off the importance of any innocent bystanders who got hurt in the process. "McCarthy's blunderbuss, loaded with rock-salt, birdshot, and nuts and bolts … is almost bound to bring down several important Reds and spies even though a few comparatively innocent people may get some rock-salt in their hides," rationalized the American Legion.[16]

For his part, McCarthy repeatedly characterized himself as an American patriot who could not worry about hurting people's feelings. "There are those who honestly say, 'Oh, we think that you are on the right track, McCarthy, and we like the results you are getting, but we don't like your methods,'" he said at one point. "Ladies and gentlemen, take my word for it…. Either I have to do a brass-knuckle job or suffer the same defeat that a vast number of well-meaning men have suffered over the past years."[17]

When these efforts to paint himself as a brave senator fighting Reds at great personal risk failed to silence all his critics, however, McCarthy returned to his preferred weapon—nasty attacks on the character and loyalty of anyone who opposed him. When Democratic senator William Benton introduced a resolution calling for McCarthy's expulsion from the Senate on the grounds that he routinely trafficked in lies and deception in August 1951, the Wisconsin senator accused Benton of being an anti-American "propagandist" and the "hero of every Communist and crook in and out of government."[18] He used similar language for members of the liberal press like cartoonist Herb Block, journalist Elmer Davis, and columnist and radio personality Drew Pearson, all of whom denounced McCarthyism as an exercise in modern-day witch hunting.

Relations between McCarthy and Pearson, who boldly criticized the morals and tactics of the senator throughout the McCarthy era, were particularly poisonous. Describing his foe as a "Moscow-directed character assassin," McCarthy organized a successful consumer boycott of the chief sponsor of Pearson's radio program. In late 1950 the senator even physically assaulted Pearson in the cloakroom at a Washington dinner club. This attack, which included several kicks to Pearson's groin, came after the journalist had endured taunts all evening from McCarthy about his plans to "ruin" him.[19] Yet none of these efforts to intimidate Pearson worked, for he remained a steadfast critic of McCarthy.

1952 Election Results Increase McCarthy's Power

In 1952 the political freight train known as McCarthyism continued to gather speed. To be sure, some opponents continued to speak out against McCarthy's tactics. They warned that his ongoing investigations were destroying the lives of innocent people. Some even asserted that he was *helping* the Communists by fostering disunity and distrust in American society. Truman remained defiant as well, charging in a speech to the conservative American Legion that McCarthy and his Red-baiting allies were ruining the country:

Journalist Drew Pearson became one of Senator McCarthy's most outspoken critics.

"They are trying to get us to believe that our Government is riddled with communism and corruption—when the fact is that we have the finest and the most loyal body of civil servants in the whole world. These slandermongers are trying to get us so hysterical that no one will stand up to them for fear of being called a Communist." The only way to halt the madness, Truman concluded, was for "every American who loves his country and his freedom … [to] take the lead against the hysteria that threatens the Government from within."[20]

McCarthy responded to these sorts of attacks with characteristic confidence. He asserted that if Truman wanted to make the fight against Communism a campaign issue in the 1952 elections, he and his fellow Republicans were bound to win. After all, McCarthy said, citizens would be faced with a choice "between Americanism and a combination of Trumanism and Communism."[21]

The Trial of the Rosenbergs

Julius and Ethel Rosenberg being returned to prison after being found guilty of treason.

After the Soviet Union detonated an atomic bomb in 1949, the FBI launched an intensive investigation to see whether the Communists had gained this knowledge through espionage. Many American physicists believed that the Russians had likely learned to make nuclear weapons on their own, but Cold War support for the investigation was high.

A few months later British investigators arrested Klaus Fuchs, a German-born scientist who had worked on the Manhattan Project—America's World War II–era nuclear weapon program—from 1944 to 1946. At the time that British agents arrested Fuchs, he was a top physicist on Britain's own nuclear project. Fuchs confessed to being a Soviet spy in January 1950, and in March he was sentenced to fourteen years in prison. The investigation did not end there, however. Fuchs told investigators that a Los Alamos technician named David Greenglass had also worked as a spy for the Soviets. In June 1950 the FBI arrested Greenglass,

McCarthy was a star attraction at the 1952 Republican Convention, where former World War II general Dwight D. Eisenhower became the party's official nominee for president. And just as he had done two years earlier, the senator from Wisconsin traveled around the country to drum up support for Republican congressional candidates. At each stop, McCarthy delivered stump speeches that emphasized the Commie-fighting determination of Republicans—and questioned the patriotism of Democratic presidential can-

who confessed to espionage and identified his sister Ethel's husband, Julius Rosenberg, as another Soviet spy. Rosenberg was arrested on July 17, but he staunchly maintained his innocence of all charges. On August 11 the U.S. government arrested Ethel as well, hoping that the prospect of seeing his wife put on trial for treason might convince Julius to confess. But both of the Rosenbergs continued to insist that they were innocent.

The trial of the Rosenbergs began on March 6, 1951. Relying almost entirely on the testimony of Greenglass, the prosecution was able to win convictions for both Julius and Ethel Rosenberg. On April 5, 1951, Judge Irving Kaufman gave both of them the death sentence for passing atomic secrets on to the Soviets (see "Julius and Ethel Rosenberg Receive Death Sentences for Treason," p. 163). This decision outraged Americans who opposed the death penalty or who believed that the Rosenbergs—and especially Ethel—were innocent. Other objections were raised on the basis that their execution would orphan their two young sons. But Kaufman's sentence was praised by millions of other Americans who believed the Rosenbergs were guilty.

Julius and Ethel Rosenberg were executed by the electric chair on June 19, 1953. The couple became the only American civilians to be executed for espionage-related activity in the entire Cold War era. Years later, decoded Soviet files from the 1950s confirmed that Julius Rosenberg did carry out espionage activities, but the guilt or innocence of Ethel Rosenberg remains a subject of continuing controversy.

Source: Radosh, Ronald, and Joyce Milton. *The Rosenberg File.* 2d ed. New Haven, CT: Yale University Press, 1997.

didate Adlai Stevenson. These lines of attack aroused some private expressions of concern from fellow Republicans like Robert Taft, the widely respected conservative senator from Ohio. But Taft and others ultimately decided that "the use of the Communist issue was a way of gaining some revenge after years in which the Democrats had portrayed Republican domestic policies as cold and heartless. Taft himself had been the target of unusually cruel assaults, which portrayed him as a pawn of the rich."[22]

As expected, the 1952 elections turned out very well for the Republicans. Eisenhower won the White House, and Republicans took control of both houses of Congress. In addition, Benton and several other dedicated foes of McCarthy were voted out of office. These changes in Washington paid immediate dividends for McCarthy. He was given chairmanship of his very own investigative body, the Permanent Subcommittee on Investigations (PSI) of the Government Operations Committee, to continue his anti-Communist crusade. McCarthy quickly appointed a staunch anti-Communist Justice Department attorney named Roy Cohn as the subcommittee's chief counsel. Cohn had attracted McCarthy's attention for his work in the 1951 espionage trial of Julius and Ethel Rosenberg, both of whom were executed in 1953 for being Soviet spies. McCarthy and Cohn quickly established a strong working relationship, and before long the lawyer was known around Washington as McCarthy's most trusted lieutenant.

The Age of McCarthyism in Full Swing

Once he received his own investigative committee, McCarthy took steps to make sure that he remained Washington's best-known anti-Communist. He called far more hearings than HUAC or any of the other congressional committees dealing with Communism at the time. In addition, McCarthy's tactics at these hearings—many of which were closed to the public—furthered his reputation as the most feared politician in America.

McCarthy targeted a few well-known writers, entertainers, and officials in these hearings. But most of the men and women who were subpoenaed to testify before McCarthy, Cohn, and the PSI were low-level clerks, secretaries, and engineers. They were in most cases ordinary Americans with left-wing political beliefs, not radicals determined to overthrow the U.S. government. McCarthy, though, spent hours grilling them about old boyfriends with alleged Communist ties, political petitions they had signed two decades earlier, or long-ago associations with "radical" labor unions.

Some of the people called to testify before McCarthy worked for the government, while others worked in the private sector. But almost all of them were terrified to be called, because they knew that they were essentially at McCarthy's mercy. The senator had the power to get them fired, turn their friends and neighbors against them, or ruin them financially through years of court battles. Even worse, McCarthy was well aware that he possessed this

In 1953 Senator Joseph McCarthy struck up a strong alliance with Roy Cohn (right), who became his chief lieutenant in the McCarthy "witch hunts."

power, and so he bullied and insulted witnesses however he pleased. As the months passed by, horror stories about McCarthy's treatment of witnesses were traded back and forth around Washington.

At times, McCarthy's committee pursued investigations of some merit. In March 1953, for example, he opened hearings on American allies who were supplying war materials to Communist China—which was at that time engaged in a war against the United States on the Korean Peninsula.[23] But many other lines of investigation were based primarily on McCarthy's own personal grudges and his thirst for the limelight. By mid-1953 the committee's three Democrats had resigned to protest McCarthy's performance as chairman. But Republican senators also stopped attending, in part because of McCarthy's habit of calling the hearings with little advance notice or far away from Washington. "As a result, McCarthy and his chief counsel Roy Cohn largely ran the show by themselves, relentlessly grilling and insulting witnesses. Harvard law dean Ervin Griswold described McCarthy's role as 'judge, jury, prosecutor, castigator, and press agent, all in one.'"[24]

McCarthy's love for publicity, however, ensured that he did not spend all his time chairing closed hearings. To the contrary, he remained an enthusiastic giver of speeches and interviews. In almost every case, the reporters who covered his statements went away with plenty of material guaranteed to sell newspapers or attract listeners. McCarthy claimed that he knew the names of hundreds of Communists working in the publishing, radio, and film industries. Even though he never released the names, the mere fact that he claimed to have a list was enough to send ripples of excitement and anxiety through America. The senator also told reporters that he had acquired evidence that several congressional aides were Communists. As usual, he never identified them or released his "evidence." But his statements alone were enough to further chill the atmosphere in Washington. "[McCarthy] had really frightened people," recalled one Senate staffer from that era. "It … just scared the hell out of me. I'm still haunted by that period." Another aide who worked in Congress during McCarthy's reign remarked that "ultimately he would send anybody to the guillotine just to get himself a headline."[25]

Even President Eisenhower was reluctant to get in McCarthy's way. Eisenhower frequently expressed outright loathing for McCarthy in private, and he nearly issued statements criticizing the senator and his "witch hunts" on several occasions. But each time, political advisors convinced him that doing so would hurt the Republican Party. So Eisenhower continued to bite his tongue, even after the press began to insinuate that McCarthy was the real leader of the party. By the fall of 1953, when the senator announced that he intended to investigate Communist infiltration of the U.S. Army, it appeared that McCarthy was unstoppable.

Notes

[1] Morgan, Ted. *Reds: McCarthyism in Twentieth-Century America.* New York: Random House, 2003, p. 375.

[2] Wicker, Tom. *Shooting Star: The Brief Arc of Joe McCarthy.* New York: Harcourt, 2006, p. 187.

[3] *Town Hall Meeting of the Air,* April 3, 1947, p. 7. Reprinted in Fried, Albert. *McCarthyism: The Great American Red Scare: A Documentary History.* New York: Oxford University Press, 1996, p. 76.

[4] Wicker, p. 9.

[5] Oshinsky, David M. *A Conspiracy So Immense: The World of Joe McCarthy.* New York: Free Press, 1983, p. 141.

[6] Truman Veto Message on the McCarran Internal Security Act (Subversive Activities Control Act) of 1950—*Public Papers of the Presidents.* Available online at http://www.trumanlibrary.org/public papers/index.php?pid=883&st=&st1=.

[7] Fried, Richard M. *Nightmare in Red: The McCarthy Era in Perspective.* New York: Oxford University Press, 1991, p. 126.

[8] Johnson, Haynes. *The Age of Anxiety: McCarthyism to Terrorism.* New York: Harcourt, 2005, pp. 124-28.

[9] Quoted in Oshinsky, p. 164.

[10] Smith, Margaret Chase. *Declaration of Conscience.* Garden City, NJ: Doubleday, 1972, pp. 13-14.

[11] Quoted in Byrd, Robert C. *The Senate, 1789-1989: Classic Speeches, 1830-1993.* Washington, DC: Government Printing Office, 1994.

[12] Quoted in Stone, Geoffrey R. "Free Speech in the Age of McCarthy: A Cautionary Tale." *California Law Review,* October 2005, p. 1387.

[13] Quoted in Fried, p. 89.

[14] Quoted in Johnson, p. 206.

[15] Quoted in Griffith, Robert. *The Politics of Fear: Joseph R. McCarthy and the Senate.* 1970. Rev. ed. Amherst: University of Massachusetts Press, 1987, p. 72.

[16] Quoted in Johnson, p. 194.

[17] Quoted in Oshinsky, p. 207.

[18] Quoted in Griffith, p. 159.

[19] *Drew Pearson Diaries, 1949-1959.* Edited by Tyler Abell. New York: Holt, Rinehart and Winston, 1974.

[20] Truman, Harry S. Address at the Dedication of the New Washington Headquarters of the American Legion, August 14, 1951. *Public Papers of the Presidents: Harry S. Truman, 1951.* Washington, DC: Government Printing Office, 1952, p. 191.

[21] Quoted in Herman, Arthur. *Joseph McCarthy: Reexamining the Life and Legacy of America's Most Hated Senator.* New York: Free Press, 1999, p. 181.

[22] Halberstam, David. *The Fifties.* New York: Villard Books, 1993, p. 57.

[23] Herman, p. 223.

[24] "June 9, 1954: Have You No Sense of Decency?" Senate Historical Office, n.a. http://www.senate.gov /artandhistory/history/minute/Have_you_no_sense_of_decency.htm.

[25] Quoted in Johnson, pp. 229-30.

Chapter Four

THE IMPACT OF MCCARTHYISM ON AMERICAN LIFE

All I can say is [when deciding to blacklist actors] there were no differentiations made between Communists, Communist sympathizers, those who had lunch with Communist sympathizers, those who knew somebody who had lunch with Communist sympathizers, and so forth.... In certain cases it even—I'm ashamed to say—included the elimination of people from shows because they had the same name as members of the Communist Party.

—Hollywood producer Mark Goodson

As Senator Joseph McCarthy's anti-Communist crusade intensified, American insecurities and fears also escalated. Convinced by McCarthy and his allies in government and the press that Communist agents and Communist sympathizers were operating in American universities, labor unions, and the U.S. government, people became more distrustful of their neighbors, church leaders, schoolteachers, librarians, and political leaders than they had ever been before. Many of these Americans ignored—or even defended—instances in which the hunt for Communists violated the constitutional rights of fellow Americans.

Meanwhile, countless other Americans rejected McCarthy's claims that treacherous "Reds" lurked in every corner of American society. But they hesitated to express opposition to McCarthy or voice any other controversial political beliefs out of fears that they too might be branded as "disloyal." They knew that in the early 1950s, many people whose background or political ideology came under suspicion were losing their jobs, friends, reputations, and—in some cases—freedom.

Government Service during the McCarthy Era

Perhaps the most high-profile institution in American society to be affected by the Red Scare of the late 1940s and early 1950s was the U.S. government itself. Ever since the founding of the United States, men and women who decided to pursue careers in government service could generally count on stable, safe, and secure jobs. During the early Cold War and McCarthy eras, however, employment in many government agencies became fraught with peril. Workers ranging from agency heads and diplomats to clerks and typists operated under a cloud of fear. Every day they woke up wondering if their department would be the next one to attract the hostile attention of anti-Communist committees in Washington.

Some influential diplomats and officials believed that such investigations were necessary—though many of them also later admitted that McCarthy's "witch hunts" went too far. According to the influential Cold War analyst and diplomat George Kennan, "penetration of the American governmental services by members or agents (conscious or otherwise) of the American Communist Party in the late 1930s was not a figment of the imagination of the hysterical right-wingers.... It really existed and assumed proportions which, while never overwhelming, were also not trivial."[1]

But while Cold War officials and historians have had spirited debates about whether Reds (Communists and Socialists) in the U.S. government posed much of a threat, they widely agree that the campaigns to "smoke them out" took a heavy toll on the morale of many innocent federal workers. In the summer of 1950, for example, the magazine *American Scholar* published a survey of employee reaction to the Truman loyalty program. According to the survey's findings, government agencies were becoming paralyzed by the "fear of ideas and of irresponsible and unknown informers." The survey's authors also reported that "government employees are afraid to attend meetings of politically minded groups; they are afraid to read 'liberal' publications; they screen their friends carefully for 'left-wing' ideas. Government employees are in very real danger of dying intellectually and politically."[2]

The working environment became even more toxic after McCarthy arrived on the scene. This deterioration was especially evident in agencies like the State Department, the nation's most important agency on foreign policy and diplomacy issues. McCarthy, Hoover, and other "Red-hunters" in Washington hammered and investigated the State Department and its Foreign

Senator Joseph McCarthy's investigations of the State Department had a major impact on agency morale and performance.

Service operations on such a relentless basis that agency officials found it harder and harder to retain or attract talented employees. Many prospective workers chose instead to pursue careers outside of government, where they would be less likely to have their life history become the subject of an FBI investigation. The situation eventually became so bad that in January 1954, five distinguished ex-diplomats (including former U.S. ambassadors to Japan, Spain, and Italy) publicly warned in a letter to the *New York Times* that McCarthyites were endangering the nation:

> The Foreign Service has been subjected to a series of attacks from outside sources which have questioned the loyalty and the moral standards of its members. With rare exceptions ... these attacks have been so flimsy as to have no standing in a court of law or in the mind of any individual capable of differentiating repeated accusation from even a reasonable presumption of

guilt. The conclusion has become inescapable ... that a Foreign Service officer who reports on persons and events to the very best of his ability and who makes recommendations which at the time he conscientiously believes to be in the interest of the United States may subsequently find his loyalty and integrity challenged and may even be forced out of the service and discredited forever as a private citizen after many years of distinguished service. A premium therefore has been put upon reporting and upon recommendations which are ambiguously stated or so cautiously set forth as to be deceiving.... The ultimate result is a threat to national security.[3]

But while investigations of the State Department garnered most of the news headlines, other government agencies and programs also received heavy attention from J. Edgar Hoover. It was his Federal Bureau of Investigation (FBI) that was responsible for conducting most of the investigations desired by McCarthy and other investigative committee chairmen in Washington. By 1953 the FBI had conducted more than 26,000 field investigations under the authority of Truman's 1947 executive order authorizing loyalty programs for federal employment. By that same time it had gathered more than 100,000 informants across the country and carried out nearly 24,000 break-ins of the offices and homes of suspects. Many of those break-ins were conducted without legal search warrants.[4]

Conformity in the Workplace and on Campus

McCarthyism also had a major impact on job security in the private sector. Suspected Communists in all sorts of industries were kicked out of their jobs during the late 1940s and 1950s. Some major employers, including General Motors and General Electric, even adopted policies in which workers who invoked the Fifth Amendment in official testimony were automatically fired. Since the Fifth Amendment was a Constitutional protection, these companies generally cited other justifications for cutting loose workers who "hid" behind it. But everyone involved understood exactly why the worker was being fired.

Industry programs to root out undesirable employees convinced many of those who survived the purgings to keep quiet about their political or social beliefs. Indeed, the dismissal of a single worker was often enough to silence an entire department full of employees. "Ten thousand people may

"You Read Books, Eh?"
—A 1962 Herblock cartoon, copyright by The Herb Block Foundation

This 1949 cartoon by Herb Block (known as Herblock) depicts a horde of "anti-subversive" investigators intimidating a school teacher. The investigator leaning on the desk with the cigar suspiciously states, "You read books, eh?"

An American Communist
Defends Using the Fifth Amendment

Writer Howard Fast had a thriving career as a screenwriter and novelist until 1950, when he was called before the House Un-American Activities Committee (HUAC). By the time of this appearance before HUAC, Fast had been an active member of the Communist Party for several years. But when asked by his interrogators whether he was a Communist, Fast refused to answer. Instead, he repeatedly cited the Fifth Amendment in the Bill of Rights, which gives every American the legal right to refuse to testify against himself or herself in a criminal case. Fast also refused to cooperate when investigators demanded to know the names of his Communist associates.

Fast ended up spending three months in prison on contempt-of-Congress charges, and he endured years of blacklisting in the publishing industry. But he remained defiant throughout this period. In 1954 he even published an essay in which he strongly defended his use of the Fifth Amendment before HUAC:

> The Communist who declares he is a Communist finds that his life has become both complex and dangerous. If he lives in the state of Pennsylvania, such a statement can result in a twenty-year prison sentence.... If he is a resident of California, local law can sentence him almost indefinitely for the same admission....

have lost their jobs," explained historian Ellen Schrecker. "Is that few or many? It may well be useful to reflect on an earlier debate among historians about the applications of sanctions—in this case the apparently low number of whippings administered under slavery—to realize that it may not be necessary to whip many slaves to keep the rest of the plantation in line."[5]

Teachers and librarians in schools and universities were hit particularly hard by the anti-Communist hysteria enveloping the country. Local and state politicians in many parts of the United States insisted that schoolteachers take loyalty oaths to keep their jobs. During this same period, school librarians and public librarians were frequently cross-examined by local authorities or conservative groups like the American Legion and Daughters of the American

The McCarran Act provides means for keeping him in prison ten years. The Smith Act, as we have already seen in a number of federal courts, can be used as a mechanism to sentence him to prison for as long as five years. But a vengeance even more immediate than the above would be visited upon any Communist Party member who answered, *yes, he was a Communist and proud of it*. The record … shows that such a person would immediately be asked to provide the names of every other Communist he knew or had heard of or had ever met with, the places where he met with them, and the substance of what was spoken of or decided upon at these meetings.

In addition, Fast noted that anyone who admitted to being Communist would no longer be allowed to invoke the Fifth Amendment: "His previous waiver of the privilege of the Fifth Amendment would destroy his subsequent use of the privilege. Therefore, his unwillingness to become a stoolpigeon, a police informer, would be rewarded with a year in prison for contempt of Congress, and fines which could be as high as $10,000. Any one of our federal kangaroo courts could also very easily— as they have in the past—construe his unwillingness to answer the question as a result of conspiracy, and add many more years of prison to the congressional sentence of one year."

Source: Fast, Howard. "Why the Fifth Amendment?" *Masses and Mainstream*, February 1954, pp. 44-50.

Revolution to make sure that their book and magazine collections did not contain "dangerous" or "radical" materials. Hundreds of elementary and high school teachers and librarians lost their jobs as a result of these investigations.

McCarthyism also triggered extensive efforts to ban or censor books and other reading materials. State legislators in Nebraska passed a law that not only required every school district to inspect textbooks for "foreign ideas," but also forced them to reserve hours of school time for the singing of patriotic songs.[6] Educators in a number of cities also reported that some factual information, such as materials describing New Deal legislation and other liberal policy priorities, was challenged as "un-American" by McCarthyite lawmakers and activists.[7] The State Department, meanwhile, sent its overseas departments lists of controversial books that they should avoid stocking on their library shelves.

> *"The taint of Communism was like a contagious disease,"* wrote McCarthy scholar Ellen Schrecker. *"Almost every survivor of the McCarthy years—Communist and political innocent alike—has a story of someone crossing the street to avoid eye contact."*

In June 1953 it briefly appeared that President Dwight Eisenhower, who was a Republican like McCarthy, was prepared to lead a counterattack against this surge in book censorship. At a June 14 commencement address at Dartmouth College, he stated: "Don't join the book-burners. Don't think you are going to conceal faults by concealing evidence that they ever existed. Don't be afraid to go in your library and read every book as long as that document does not offend your sense of decency. That should be the only censorship."[8] Three days later, however, Eisenhower backtracked by claiming that there were some circumstances in which book burning and censorship was acceptable. This reversal left defenders of free speech even more depressed than they had been before the president's remarks at Dartmouth.

The impact of all these acts of intimidation, censorship, and demands for conformity was also evident on America's college campuses. After three tenured professors at the University of Washington were fired in 1948 for alleged Communist backgrounds, a wave of similar dismissals of faculty members took place across the country. Few of these professors were dismissed for being Communists. Rather, most lost their jobs after refusing to sign university loyalty oaths or after taking the Fifth Amendment when called before congressional or university committees. Many of the men and women who lost their jobs in the latter manner were ex-Communists who refused to "name names"—reveal the identities of old friends and colleagues to investigators. These academic purges took place in both private and public schools, but they were most commonplace in public universities that relied on funding from anti-Communist state lawmakers.[9]

Virtually none of the professors who were dismissed for political reasons during the McCarthy era were ever accused of slanting their scholarly work in a pro-Communist way or of indoctrinating their students with "anti-American" ideas. But the slightest association with Communism or other left-wing political views was still enough to kill careers. Not surprisingly, then, professors and high school teachers alike became extremely reluctant to discuss Communism in their classrooms in *any* capacity. And in the end, this muffling of American education and knowledge-seeking hurt students as much as anyone.

Paul Hoffman, who served as chairman of the Studebaker-Packard car company, recalled that after he delivered an address on freedom to an audience of college students, a student approached him and asked: "Do you think there ought to be any study of communism in a school such as this?"

"Yes," Hoffman responded. "I think we ought to teach what communism *is*, so that the new and most important generation of Americans can know exactly why it is such a menace to our way of life."

"I think so too," the student said, "but it's dangerous to say that around here now."[10]

The changed atmosphere on campuses was not sufficient, however, to satisfy Americans who accepted McCarthy's view of universities as hotbeds of anti-patriotic, pro-Communist sentiment. Suspicious and frightened, these men and women stopped seeing universities as citadels of intellectual freedom and learning and started seeing them as threats to the American way of life. In fact, Goldman observed that many Americans of this era began using the word "intellectual" as if it "meant some compound of evil, stupidity, and treason."[11]

American Media Cower in the Face of McCarthyism

The American news media and popular culture were also profoundly affected by McCarthyism. During the Red Scare of the late 1940s and McCarthy's rise to power in the early 1950s, a handful of reporters, columnists, and commentators issued repeated warnings about the excesses of McCarthyism. The most prominent anti-McCarthyism journalists included Drew Pearson, Mary McGrory, Walter Lippmann, Joseph and Stewart Alsop, Elmer Davis, Martin Agronsky, I. F. Stone, and Herbert "Herblock" Block. Some of these men and women spoke from a conservative political orientation, while others were far more liberal. But all of them urged their readers and viewers to think for themselves and to resist the hysteria and fear that the worst Red-hunters were churning up in American communities.

These bold voices, however, were largely drowned out by the soft, uncritical coverage provided by many other journalists and news outlets. Eager to boost their circulation and increase their advertising revenue, newspapers, magazines, and radio and television news programs frequently passed along McCarthy's most outrageous smears and innuendos without hesitation. "The real scandal," charged the famous journalist David Halberstam many years later, "was the behavior of the members of the Washington press corps, who, more often than not, knew better. They were delighted to be a part of [McCarthy's] traveling road show, chronicling each charge and then moving on to the next town, instead of bothering to stay behind to follow up. They had little interest in reporting how careless he was or how little it all meant to him. It was news and he was news; that was all that mattered."[12]

Meanwhile, producers of American popular culture displayed extreme caution in their operations. Radio and television studios and networks avoided any programming that had the slightest chance of sparking political controversy. Instead, they fed their audiences a steady diet of lighthearted comedies, quiz shows, and Westerns. Hollywood displayed even greater fears about being labeled as soft on Communism or otherwise "un-American" (see "Ronald Reagan Assesses Hollywood's Progress against the Reds," p. 166). With the memories of the Hollywood Ten episode still fresh in their minds, most movie executives stayed away from any scriptwriters, actors, directors, or storylines that had the potential to anger McCarthy and his allies. In fact, Hollywood went so far as to release thirteen films with clear anti-Communist messages in 1952 alone. As film scholar Dorothy Jones later remarked, "Probably never before in the history of Hollywood had such a large number of films been produced which the industry itself doubted would prove really profitable at the box office."[13]

There were a few notable exceptions to this general timidity. An early-1950s science fiction television show called *The Twilight Zone* featured several episodes that took thinly veiled shots at McCarthyism. In 1956 Columbia Pictures released *Storm Center,* in which actress Bette Davis portrayed a heroic small-town librarian who refuses to pull a Communist book off the shelves, even though her stand against censorship leads the community to falsely brand her as a Communist. This film, which a nervous Columbia released only after several delays, was the first Hollywood film to explicitly criticize McCarthyism. American writers, meanwhile, produced numerous novels, essays, and plays condemning McCarthy and "the Great Fear" he was fomenting across the country. The most famous of the era's anti-McCarthy works was Arthur Miller's 1953 play *The Crucible,* which used Massachusetts's Salem Witch Trials of 1692 as a parable for McCarthyism (see "Playwright Arthur Miller Recalls the McCarthy Era," p. 187).

A scene from the 1953 Broadway production of Arthur Miller's anti-McCarthyism play *The Crucible.*

These brave stands, however, did little to calm Americans who had fallen under the spell of McCarthyism. In many parts of the country, even the smallest incident was enough to set off a fit of hysterical overreaction. In 1952, for example, a policeman in Wheeling, West Virginia—where McCarthy had issued the famous speech that launched him to stardom—reported that local penny-candy vending machines were dispensing candies with little geography lessons attached. One of the little geography cards was for the Soviet Union, and it included a tiny representation of the Soviet flag and basic information such as its capital city (Moscow), its population (211 million), and its status as the planet's largest country by area. The discovery of this "propaganda" caused such a fuss in Wheeling that the city manager ordered the seizure of all penny-candy machines in town. These "stern measures," as historian Eric F. Goldman mockingly called them, thus protected "the candy-store set from the knowledge that the Soviet Union existed and that it was the biggest country in the world."[14]

"The Black Silence of Fear"

As McCarthyism steadily tightened its grip around American society, prominent individuals and organizations from all corners of the country joined the uphill battle being waged against McCarthy. In January 1952, for example, Supreme Court Justice William O. Douglas set aside the Court's customary silence on political issues to deliver a stinging indictment of the "black silence of fear" that had settled across America:

> The Communist threat inside the country has been magnified and exalted far beyond its realities. Irresponsible talk by irresponsible people has fanned the flames of fear. Accusations have been loosely made. Character assassinations have become common. Suspicion has taken the place of goodwill. Once we could debate with impunity along a wide range of inquiry. Once we could safely explore to the edges of a problem, challenge orthodoxy without qualms, and run the gamut of ideas in search of solutions to perplexing problems. Once we had confidence in each other. Now there is suspicion. Innocent acts become telltale marks of disloyalty. The coincidence that an idea parallels Soviet Russia's policy for a moment of time settles an aura of suspicion around a person....
>
> Fear has driven more and more men and women in all walks of life either to silence or to the folds of the orthodox. Fear has mounted: fear of losing one's job, fear of being investigated, fear of being pilloried. This fear has stereotyped our thinking, narrowed the range of free public discussion, and driven many thoughtful people to despair. This fear has even entered universities, great citadels of our spiritual strength, and corrupted them. We have the spectacle of university officials lending themselves to one of the worst witch-hunts we have seen since early days.[15]

But many other groups and individuals that had a strong orientation toward the defense of freedom of speech and other civil liberties were strangely quiet or passive during the McCarthy era. Many lawyers refused to provide legal representation to accused Communists out of fear that their reputations would suffer or their other clients would object. Organizations that usually stood on the front lines of battles over constitutional rights also remained quiet. The American Civil Liberties Union (ACLU), for example, refused to get involved in specific cases—and in some cases ACLU officials even cooperated with the FBI on its investigations. Meanwhile, internal dissension and leadership struggles within the American Association of University Professors (AAUP) kept it from organizing any effective response to the firings of professors that took place across the country in the late 1940s and early 1950s.

The U.S. Supreme Court also stood on the sidelines, despite the urging of Douglas. It let many anti-Communist laws and regulations stand

Supreme Court justice William O. Douglas wrote "The Black Silence of Fear" in response to McCarthyism.

despite the fact that they violated basic constitutional rights such as freedom of speech. For the majority of Supreme Court justices, national security concerns outweighed any other considerations.

Given all of these factors, then, it is little wonder that Americans accused of subversive beliefs or activities frequently felt alone and abandoned. Some men and women targeted for investigation at least had the support of family and close friends, but even these sources of strength did not always remain steadfast in their support. Some friends and family drifted away when charges were first brought. Others faded away when prison sentences for perjury or contempt of Congress were handed down. And still others kept their distance in hopes that they could keep themselves out of the crosshairs of investigators. "The taint of Communism was like a contagious disease," wrote McCarthy scholar Ellen Schrecker. "Almost every survivor of the McCarthy years—Communist and political innocent alike—has a story of someone crossing the street to avoid eye contact."[16]

Most Americans who were targeted by McCarthy, Hoover, and other anti-Communist crusaders were law-abiding citizens, but Schrecker acknowledges that relatively few of them were victims of mistaken identity. "Most of the men and women who lost their jobs or were otherwise victimized were not apolitical folks who had somehow gotten on the wrong mailing lists or signed the wrong petitions," she wrote. "Rather ... they had once been in or near the American Communist party. Whether or not they should have been victimized, they certainly were not misidentified. But they were stigmatized, portrayed as members of an illegal conspiracy that somehow threatened America's very existence. Stereotypes prevailed, turning individual Communists into alien beings whose destruction was, therefore, easy to justify."[17]

The terror and humiliation of being investigated by McCarthy and other congressional inquisitors took a heavy toll. Many marriages and friendships buckled under the strain. Some targets fled underground to avoid prosecution. Others endured their circumstances with furious protests, tearful sobs, or dignified silence. And a few Americans who came under investigation were so devastated by the specter of ruined reputations, imprisonments, or deportations that they sought to end their suffering by taking their own lives.

Notes

[1] Kennan, George F. *Memoirs: 1950-1963.* New York: Atlantic Monthly Press, 1972, p. 191.

[2] Nikoloric, L.A. "The Government Loyalty Program," *American Scholar,* Summer 1950.

[3] "National Affairs: A Yellow Light." *Time,* January 25, 1954.

[4] Leebaert, Derek. *The Fifty-Year Wound: How America's Cold War Victory Shapes Our World.* Boston: Back Bay Books, 2002, p. 111.

[5] Schrecker, Ellen. *The Age of McCarthyism: A Brief History with Documents.* Boston: St. Martin's Press, 1994, p. 92.

[6] Johnson, Haynes. *The Age of Anxiety: McCarthyism to Terrorism.* New York: Harcourt, 2005, p. 169-70.

[7] Goldman, Eric F. *The Crucial Decade—and After: America, 1945-1960.* New York: Vintage Books, 1960, p. 215.

[8] Quoted in Wicker, Tom. *Dwight D. Eisenhower.* New York: Times Books, 2002, p. 59.

[9] Schrecker, Ellen. *No Ivory Tower: McCarthyism and the Universities.* New York: Oxford University Press, 1986.

[10] Quoted in Goldman, p. 259.

[11] Goldman, p. 123.

[12] Halberstam, David. *The Fifties.* New York: Villard, 1993, p. 55.

[13] Quoted in Navasky, Victor. *Naming Names.* New York: Viking Press, 1980, p. 337.

[14] Goldman, p. 213.

[15] Douglas, William O. "The Black Silence of Fear." *The New York Times Magazine,* January 13, 1952. Reprinted by permission of the Estate of William O. Douglas.

[16] Schrecker, Ellen. *Many Are the Crimes: McCarthyism in America.* Boston: Little, Brown, 1998, p. 367.

[17] Schrecker, p. xii.

Chapter Five

MCCARTHY'S STUNNING POLITICAL COLLAPSE

<hr>

Have you no sense of decency, sir, at long last? Have you left
no sense of decency?

—Army chief counsel Joseph N. Welch

For much of 1953 Senator Joseph McCarthy roared across American politics like a runaway train, sending opponents scurrying off the tracks to avoid being pulverized. Complaints about his bullying behavior and irresponsible claims were drowned out by the fearsome political power he possessed. But in 1954 McCarthy's careless, brawling style finally got him into serious trouble. And by that time he had alienated so many people in Washington—including President Dwight Eisenhower—that he could not save himself from political ruin. In fact, McCarthy's plummet from the political heights proved to be just as sudden and spectacular as his rise from obscurity had been a mere four years earlier.

Eisenhower and McCarthy

McCarthy sowed the seeds of his own destruction in 1953. During that year, McCarthy used his chairmanship of the Permanent Subcommittee on Investigations (PSI) as a free pass to investigate any individual and agency he pleased. His chief ally in these efforts remained Roy Cohn, the chief counsel for the subcommittee. McCarthy and Cohn, in fact, were often the lone PSI representatives at hearings. Democratic committee members had decided to boycott McCarthy's "witch hunts," while Republican colleagues had simply tired of the Wisconsin senator's antics.

None of this really hurt McCarthy's political standing. The American public remained generally supportive of his anti-Communist crusade, despite some misgivings about his tactics. Republican president Eisenhower also remained reluctant to confront McCarthy publicly, even though he privately regarded the senator as a loathsome bully. Eisenhower recognized that if he challenged McCarthy, the unity of the Republican Party would be threatened.

As the months passed by, however, chinks in McCarthy's armor appeared. McCarthy's alcohol consumption, which had always been high, jumped to even more alarming levels. In addition, the Eisenhower administration and many congressional Republicans became increasingly frustrated with McCarthy's never-ending Commie hunt. Back when Democrats had controlled the White House and Congress, they had happily cheered McCarthy's quest for Reds lurking in the government. But when McCarthy continued this same campaign even after Republicans had gained control of the executive and legislative branches in the 1952 elections, they grumbled that his actions threatened to embarrass the party.

> *"If a stupid, arrogant or witless man in a position of power appears before our committee and is found to be aiding the Communist party, he will be exposed,"* declared McCarthy.

Vice President Richard Nixon and other prominent Republicans quietly tried to explain all this to McCarthy, but the senator took a defiant stand. They were asking him to abandon the crusade that had made him a political star, and that was something he refused to do. Instead, McCarthy continued his relentless search for headlines. During this time, in fact, he actually widened his range of targets from the State Department, which had been his main focus during the Truman years, to the Central Intelligence Agency (CIA), the Atomic Energy Commission (AEC), the Voice of America (VOA) broadcasting service, and other government departments. He even attacked Eisenhower's nominee to be the U.S. ambassador to the Soviet Union in Moscow. These actions convinced the Eisenhower administration that the senator was out of control, and by the late summer White House officials were quietly exploring ways in which they might rid themselves of the McCarthy "problem."

Picking a Fight with the U.S. Army

In the fall of 1953 McCarthy and Cohn made a serious political miscalculation—and in the process gave the Eisenhower administration the opening it had been looking for to strike back at the senator. Earlier that year McCarthy and Cohn had hired G. David Schine, a young anti-Communist from a rich and affluent family, on to the subcommittee staff. By late summer

Washington was buzzing with speculation that Cohn and Schine were engaged in a homosexual relationship. These rumors intensified after journalist Drew Pearson revealed that Cohn and McCarthy had unsuccessfully appealed to the U.S. Army for a military commission—an officer ranking—for Schine, who was facing compulsory induction into the military.[1] Subsequent efforts to orchestrate a commission for Schine in the Navy and Air Force also failed.

In October 1953 McCarthy announced that he and Cohn had uncovered evidence of a Communist spy ring operating out of an Army Signal Corps facility in Fort Monmouth, New Jersey. In reality, though, this accusation was based on old information that had already been investigated by both the FBI and HUAC. Some observers in Washington believed that McCarthy's announcement was calculated to punish the Army for failing to provide a commission to Schine.

In early November—after several delays in his induction—Schine was finally forced to enter the U.S. Army at Fort Dix, New Jersey, with the rank of private. This development infuriated Cohn, who relentlessly lobbied Secretary of the Army Robert Stevens to give Schine light duties, extra leave, and other preferential treatment. Cohn also threatened to ruin Stevens and "wreck the army" if Schine was posted overseas.[2]

Schine received a great deal of special consideration from Army officials over the next several weeks. He was excused from guard duty and menial chores that were typically assigned to privates, he received extra passes to leave the base during the week and on weekends, and he was even given a car and driver to take him into New York on those occasions. Schine's special privileges became so obvious that the commander at Fort Dix complained to the office of Army secretary Stevens that the situation was hurting base morale.

The clashes over Schine jumped to a new level in early 1954, when Cohn and McCarthy learned that Schine was being reassigned to a base in far-away Georgia. The two men erupted with dark promises to broaden their investigation of the Army. The White House's response was to quietly order an Army official named John Adams to compile a record of all the times that Cohn had—with McCarthy's blessing—issued threats and bribes to secure special arrangements for Schine.

As Adams worked on his assignment, McCarthy seized on the case of an army dentist named Irving Peress, who had been given an honorable discharge after army investigators learned that he had concealed past Communist ties from his superiors. McCarthy and Cohn subsequently called Peress's commanding officer, General Ralph Zwicker, to testify before the PSI. As usual, McCarthy was the only senator at the hearing. As the hearing wore on, the senator insulted Zwicker's intelligence, accused the general of being soft on Communism, and declared him to be unfit for command.

McCarthy's abusive treatment of Zwicker, a general who had earned top honors on the field of battle in World War II, stunned many people in Washington. It also deeply angered many military officers and Secretary Stevens, who vowed that he would not permit any more attacks from McCarthy on his officers. Speculation ran rampant that Eisenhower, who had been a decorated World War II army general himself, might finally rebuke McCarthy publicly. Instead, to the great disappointment of McCarthy's foes, Eisenhower only issued a mild statement on March 3 reminding all members of Congress to treat people with "respect and courtesy." Even this was too much for McCarthy to take, though. He hastily called a press conference and told the assembled reporters that "if a stupid, arrogant or witless man in a position of power appears before our committee and is found to be aiding the Communist party, he will be exposed." McCarthy also assured the reporters that he remained more determined than ever to expose "those who are dedicated to the Communist enslavement of the world."[3]

McCarthy on the Ropes

McCarthy's defiance was applauded by his supporters, but it reflected a complete refusal to adjust to the fact "the McCarthy show had been playing for too long," as journalist David Halberstam put it. "Three years of endless charges with little proof were wearing thin."[4] Frustrated by McCarthy's behavior toward the Eisenhower White House and his unquenchable thirst for publicity, the senator's fellow Republicans displayed dwindling enthusiasm for defending his bullying tactics and outlandish charges. Moreover, magazines and newspapers that had once glorified McCarthy began publishing negative pieces on the senator and his "Red-baiting" ways. As journalist Andrew Ferguson later noted, this shift in tone extended even to reliably conservative news outlets of the 1950s: "Among those routinely critical were *Time* magazine and Col. Robert McCormick's *Chicago Tribune*. If Col. McCormick and [*Time* publisher] Henry Luce were denouncing a right-wing icon, you could feel pretty safe in firing away."[5]

A still image from newsman Edward R. Murrow's historic *See It Now* program on Joe McCarthy.

This downturn in support made it impossible for McCarthy to withstand the series of events that began to unfold on March 9, 1954. That day, Democratic senator Ralph Flanders of Vermont flayed McCarthy in a speech on the floor of the Senate. This verbal assault, which would have been almost unimaginable a mere year earlier, prompted Eisenhower to write Flanders an appreciative note telling him that America "needs to hear more voices like yours."[6] That same afternoon, defense secretary Charles Wilson informed McCarthy that the army intended to release its secret "Adams report" on Cohn's relentless efforts on behalf of Schine unless Cohn resigned. McCarthy's response was to tell the Army to "go to hell."[7] And later that same evening, CBS broadcast a hard-hitting report on McCarthy on *See It Now*, a news program hosted by legendary journalist Edward R. Murrow. The broadcast was condemned in some quarters as biased and unfair, but others hailed it as a long-overdue challenge. Everyone agreed that the Murrow show delivered a serious blow to McCarthy's image (see "Edward R. Murrow Takes on McCarthy," p. 169).

March 9 had been a very bad day for McCarthy and Cohn, but March 11 was even worse. That afternoon, the Pentagon finally released Adams's report on the Schine case. The report documented forty-four different occasions, from July 1953 to February 1954, in which Cohn, McCarthy, or McCarthy's staff director, Frank Carr, had used their positions to exert improper pressure on the Army regarding Schine. These revelations, coming at a time when young American soldiers *without* political connections were dying in large numbers in the Korean War, rocked Washington and dominated newspaper headlines across the country.

McCarthy answered these charges in the only way he knew how: with a counterattack. He declared that Stevens and other military officials had over the past several months repeatedly engaged in blackmail, threatening to ruin Schine if McCarthy did not suspend his investigations of the Army. The other members of McCarthy's subcommittee were skeptical of McCarthy's sudden accusation, but they recognized that they would need to conduct an inquiry to determine the truth of the matter. As a result, PSI members who had not actually participated in any of the subcommittee's hearings for weeks or even months gathered together to hold hearings on the Army-McCarthy dispute. They also told McCarthy that he would have to temporarily step down as chairman, since he could not preside over an investigation of himself. McCarthy agreed and handed the subcommittee reins over to Karl Mundt of South Dakota, a conservative Republican who remained a steadfast supporter of McCarthy.

The Army-McCarthy Hearings

When the so-called Army-McCarthy hearings convened on April 22, 1954, the Senate Caucus Room was packed with lawyers, journalists, spectators, and network cameramen. The clash, in fact, turned out to be an early landmark in television history. Of the four television networks operating at that time, CBS and NBC provided only nightly summaries of the action from the hearings. But ABC and Dumont (a smaller network that folded in 1955) aired the entirety of the hearings, which played out over a total of thirty-six days. ABC's decision gave the network a ratings bonanza, as huge numbers of Americans tuned in for the courtroom drama.

In 1954 Senator Joe McCarthy (center) and two aides, G. David Schine (left) and Roy Cohn (right), became involved in a fierce clash with the U.S. Army.

The hearings went badly for McCarthy and Cohn from the start. Army chief counsel Joseph Welch and his legal team called multiple witnesses who convincingly testified about what Secretary Stevens called a "persistent, tireless effort" from Cohn and McCarthy "to obtain special consideration and privileges" for Schine. McCarthy managed to expose Stevens as an overly cautious and confrontation-averse administrator in cross-examination, but he was unable to shake Stevens's damaging testimony. Later in the trial, McCarthy and Cohn introduced manuscripts and photographs that they described as evidence of Army treachery in the Schine case. But Welch's team proved that this "evidence" had been forged or doctored, which further weakened McCarthy's hand.

Worst of all, though, ABC's television coverage provided Americans with an extended opportunity to judge McCarthy for themselves. And McCarthy, who suffered from headaches and bouts of upset stomach throughout the hearings (probably as a result of his escalating alcohol abuse), did not benefit from the spotlight. "Prolonged exposure to McCarthy's odious character and ill-mannered interruptions was a textbook demonstration of how a hot personality wilted under the glare of a cool medium," wrote historian Thomas Doherty. "Toward the close of the hearings, Senator Stuart Symington (Democrat, Missouri) underscored the lesson in media politics during a sharp exchange with McCarthy: 'The American people have had a look at you for six weeks. You are not fooling anyone.'"[8]

The final, crucial blow to McCarthy's sinking career came on June 9. The desperate senator charged that a young associate in Welch's law firm had once belonged to the left-wing National Lawyers Guild, which McCarthy viewed as a Communist front organization. Welch responded with a withering speech that was instantly broadcast to millions of watching Americans. "Until this moment, senator, I think I never really gauged your cruelty or your recklessness," Welch stated, then pushed on with a defense of the young lawyer that ended with a devastating dig at McCarthy. "Let us not assassinate this lad further, senator. You have done enough. Have you no sense of decency, sir, at long last? Have you left no sense of decency?"[9]

Historians have long debated whether Welch had anticipated McCarthy's line of attack and prepared a response in advance, but in the final analysis it does not matter. Either way, Welch's reply was a final crowning blow to McCarthy's fast-fading political fortunes (see "The Army-McCarthy Hearings Bring McCarthy Down," p. 178). The Army-McCarthy hearings extended for another eight days before permanently adjourning, but these sessions were anticlimactic. The damage had already been done.

When McCarthy emerged from the hearings he found a changed political landscape. "McCarthy has become a major liability to the cause of anti-Communism," pronounced the influential anti-Communist journalist Frederick Woltman in a scathing assessment that was published in newspapers across the country in July. Woltman decried the senator's "reckless, knee-to-the-groin tactics which violate our sense of fair play" and charged that "the McCarthy strategy of 'you're either for me or a friend of the Communists' is … a boon to the Communists."[10] Many other Americans agreed. The Gallup

U.S. Army counsel Joseph Welch (left) highlighted the unsavory Red-baiting tactics of Joe McCarthy (right) throughout the Army-McCarthy hearings.

Poll organization reported that from January 1954 to June 1954, McCarthy's national favorability ratings had taken a nose dive. The percentage of Americans who viewed him favorably had fallen from 50 percent to 34 percent. Meanwhile, the percentage who gave him unfavorable marks had jumped from 29 percent to 45 percent. "Whether he was seen as a dangerous demagogue or as a national hero, McCarthy like Humpty Dumpty [had taken] a great fall," wrote biographer Tom Wicker. "And after those fatal 188 hours in 1954 he never put himself together again."[11]

The Senate Rebukes McCarthy

McCarthy's opponents recognized that they finally possessed the power to take him on. The first Senate resolution to punish McCarthy for his many transgressions was introduced by Flanders on June 11, six days before the Army-McCarthy hearings even ended. In August Flanders reintroduced his resolution, which called on the Senate to "censure"—officially rebuke and condemn—the Wisconsin senator for his behavior over the previous several years. Support for the resolution was enhanced by the August 31 release of the final PSI report on the Army-McCarthy hearings, which confirmed the widespread belief that McCarthy and Cohn had abused their positions in seeking special treatment for Schine.

In September a Senate subcommittee known as the Watkins Committee unanimously endorsed Flanders's resolution to censure McCarthy. The subcommittee formally called for censuring for two offenses: repeated acts of "contempt" for the Senate in 1951-52, when Benton's resolution to expel McCarthy had been under consideration; and his "reprehensible" treatment of General Zwicker in early 1954. No mention was made of the senator's central role in spreading McCarthyism across the land, nor of his actions on behalf of Schine.

The exact language of the resolution changed over the next several weeks in order to garner the broadest possible support for the bill. The charges regarding Zwicker and Benton were dropped, but new language that condemned McCarthy for his criticisms of the Watkins Committee was added. A full Senate vote on the resolution was finally taken on December 2, 1954, and it passed by a resounding 67-22 count. The 67 senators who voted against McCarthy included 44 Democrats, 22 Republicans (mostly from eastern and northern states), and one independent. McCarthy himself just voted "present" and six senators were absent from the vote (see "The Senate Condemns McCarthy," p. 185).

In the wake of this humiliating scolding, McCarthy became almost a ghost in Washington. The return of a Democratic majority to the Senate in the 1954 elections meant that his days as a committee chairman were over. With his power greatly reduced, McCarthy tried to recapture his once-huge following by issuing new anti-Communist speeches. But these speeches were widely ignored, both by fellow senators and by reporters who had once hung on his every word. As Eisenhower himself said, "It's no longer McCarthyism. It's McCarthywasm."[12]

McCarthy's descent into disgrace made him even more dependent on alcohol. His drinking became so heavy that he was hospitalized several times, and senators and aides encountered a visibly inebriated McCarthy in the Sen-

Democrat William Proxmire won the special senatorial election held in Wisconsin after Joe McCarthy's death in 1957.

ate building on a number of occasions. On April 28, 1957, he was admitted to Bethesda Naval Hospital in Maryland in failing health. He died on May 2 of acute hepatitis of the liver, a direct result of his struggles with alcoholism. Wisconsin subsequently held a special senate election to replace him, on August 28, 1957. The victor in this contest was Democrat William Proxmire, who represented Wisconsin in the U.S. Senate for the next 32 years.

After McCarthy's death, few of his adversaries offered any commentary on his life apart from the usual condolences to his surviving family. Since then, however, a strong historical consensus has emerged about McCarthy and his controversial career. This consensus was aptly summarized by historian Paul Johnson, who wrote that "McCarthy was never a serious investigator of subversion but a politician trying to draw attention to himself. He was first amazed, then unbalanced, and finally destroyed by his success. There is no evidence he ever identified any subversive not already known to the authorities and the only consequence of his activities was to cause trouble and distress for a lot of innocent people and discredit the activities of those genuinely concerned to make America safe."[13]

Notes

[1] Wicker, Tom. *Shooting Star: The Brief Arc of Joe McCarthy.* New York: Harcourt, 2006, p. 135.

[2] Quoted in Morgan, Ted. *Reds: McCarthyism in Twentieth-Century America.* New York: Random House, 2003, p. 468.

[3] Oshinsky, David M. *A Conspiracy So Immense: The World of Joe McCarthy.* New York: Free Press, 1983, pp. 390-92.

[4] Halberstam, David. *The Fifties.* New York: Villard, 1993, pp. 55-56

[5] Quoted in Shafer, Jack. "Good Night, and Good Luck and Bad History." *Slate,* October 5, 2005. Available online at http://www.slate.com/id/2127595/.

[6] Quoted in Morgan, p. 476.

[7] Oshinsky, p. 400.

[8] Quoted in Doherty, Thomas. "The Army-McCarthy Hearings: U.S. Congressional Inquiry." *Museum of Broadcast Communications.* Available online at http://www.museum.tv/eotvsection.php?entry code=army-mccarthy.

[9] "McCarthy Hearings, 1954." U.S. Senate Historical Office. Available online at www.senate.gov/art andhistory/history/common/generic/News McCarthy Hearings.htm.

[10] Quoted in "An Expert Rating of McCarthy," *LIFE,* July 26, 1954, p. 20.

[11] Wicker, p. 164.

[12] Quoted in Morgan, p. 505.

[13] Johnson, Paul. *A History of the American People.* New York: HarperPerennial, 1999, p. 835.

Chapter Six

THE LEGACY OF
THE MCCARTHY ERA

More than a half century has passed since Joseph McCarthy walked the halls of the U.S. Senate, and the phenomenon known as McCarthyism is now treated by most Americans as an embarrassing but long-concluded moment in the nation's history. But McCarthyism continued to reverberate in American politics and society long after the 1950s drew to a close. In addition, Americans today are engaged in fierce political debates about whether twenty-first-century versions of McCarthyism now stalk the land.

Lessons of McCarthyism

In the years immediately following McCarthy's fall from grace and the decline in concern about Communism across America, most attention was placed on what historian Ellen Schrecker termed the "human wreckage" of McCarthyism: "From Hollywood to Harvard, the anticommunist crusade blighted thousands of lives, careers, and marriages. People's experiences varied, as did their reactions to them. Some folks flourished; others were destroyed; most managed to survive. They all experienced stress."[1] Taking stock of this terrible damage, Americans of all different walks of life and political views vowed that they would never allow the nation to again be swallowed up in such ugly paranoia or show such disregard for constitutional rights.

Some Democrats were so spooked by the political beating they took during the Red Scare of the late 1940s and 1950s that they spent the rest of the century trying to prove to American voters that they hated Communism just as much as the Republicans.

Other lessons were learned during the McCarthy era as well, and some of them were hurtful to America. During the 1950s and 1960s, for example, white segregationists in the Deep South took a page from McCarthyism and used Red-baiting to smear leaders of the civil rights movement. Martin Luther King Jr. and other activists were repeatedly accused of being "Reds"—Socialist or Communist agitators—by segregationists who did not want to acknowledge that their opposition was really based on racist beliefs. This effort to ward off the civil rights movement through McCarthyite tactics ultimately failed—but it did make the transition to an integrated society much more difficult in many areas of the country.

America's political left, meanwhile, was traumatized for decades by McCarthyism. When the anti-Communist crusades of the 1940s and 1950s obliterated virtually all traces of organized Communist activity in America, the left lost one of the most energetic elements of its political coalition. Their absence was particularly evident in the labor movement, which had purged itself of most Communist and Socialist elements during the 1940s. This weeding out of Reds was undertaken in an effort to convince lawmakers and the public that the unions were filled with "loyal Americans," but it weakened the solidarity and strength of a number of unions. Put on the defensive by McCarthyism—and by corporations that had regained their confidence and financial vitality during World War II—the labor movement was unable to hold off the Taft-Hartley Act of 1947 or other anti-union legislation that followed in subsequent decades.

Similarly, years after McCarthyism had faded from newspaper headlines, mainstream liberals remained leery of pursuing political goals that might be painted by opponents as "radical" or "un-American." This caution slowed liberal efforts to establish programs of national health insurance and financial assistance to the elderly and the unemployed in the United States, even as many other industrialized nations went ahead and passed such measures.

Some of these liberal measures finally passed in the 1960s, when America went through an extended period of political liberalism. The Medicare Act of 1965, for example, established a sweeping new program of federal help for senior citizens. But other liberal policy goals—such as the implementation of a

Historians believe that Democratic fears about being labeled as "soft" on Communism played a big role in America's military and foreign policy—especially on the Vietnam War.

system for national health insurance—failed to get the necessary political and popular support. To be sure, some of the opposition to national health insurance proposals was based on legitimate concerns that passage would mean higher taxes or increased government intrusions into the personal and business affairs of Americans. Conservatives voiced these objections repeatedly and with genuine feeling. But opponents also acted on the knowledge that affixing the "Red" stamp on *any* piece of liberal legislation remained the single most effective way of draining public support for it. "All you have to do is give [national health insurance] a bad name, and have a Devil," acknowledged one public relations executive who was heavily involved in the campaign to stop national health insurance in the post-war era. "America's opposed to socialism so we're going to name national health insurance 'socialized medicine.'"[2]

The McCarthy era also shaped the foreign policy of the United States—and the foreign affairs perspectives of Democrats and Republicans—for the rest of the twentieth century. In the 1960s, for example, Cold War fears about a world ruled by Communism led the United States into the Vietnam War, a complex conflict that ultimately claimed the lives of more than 58,000 American soldiers and millions of Vietnamese people and soldiers. Some analysts, historians, and government officials believe that America's entrance into the war to ward off a Communist takeover of South Vietnam stemmed to a large degree from a State Department that still bore the wounds of McCarthyism. The agency had dismissed some of its most experienced Asia experts during the McCarthy era for alleged Communist sympathies. If these analysts had still been in place, they might have convinced American military leaders and policymakers that involvement in Vietnam was a mistake. In the meantime, those employees who remained at the State Department were extremely reluctant to provide any analysis that might open them to charges that they were "soft" on Communism.

Presidents learned this lesson as well. Years after Democratic president Lyndon B. Johnson dramatically widened American involvement in Vietnam in the mid-1960s, he admitted that he approved an expansion of the war because he knew that a Communist takeover of all of Vietnam would spark "an endless national debate—a mean and destructive debate—that would shatter my Presidency, kill my administration, and damage our democracy. I knew that Harry Truman and Dean Acheson had lost their effectiveness from the day that the Communists took over in China. I believed that the loss of China had played a large role in the rise of Joe McCarthy."[3]

Some Democrats, like Johnson, were so spooked by the political beating they took during the Red Scare of the late 1940s and 1950s that they spent the rest of the century trying to prove to American voters that they hated Communism just as much as the Republicans. This state of affairs benefited the Republican Party on the whole, but it made it difficult for even Republican lawmakers, officials, and analysts to pursue foreign policy strategies that might be construed as insufficiently "tough" towards Communist or Socialist threats. As Schrecker observed, "the memories of the damage inflicted by McCarthy and his colleagues limited the options that policymakers felt able to exercise."[4]

American Media and Popular Culture after McCarthy

Most of America's far-flung entertainment industry underwent a gradual recovery from the McCarthy witch hunts. In the film, television, and radio

Actor David Strathairn as Edward R. Murrow in the 2005 film *Good Night, and Good Luck.*

industries, the blacklisting of writers, actors, producers, and directors suspected of being Reds eased significantly by 1960. This return to normalcy was greatly aided by Dalton Trumbo's 1959 announcement that he had won a 1956 Academy Award for the screenplay to *The Brave One* under the name Robert Rich. Within a few years of that revelation, a number of prominent performers and artists who had suffered blacklisting were getting regular work. Still, few of them recaptured their pre-McCarthy level of success, and one authoritative study estimated that only one out of ten people who were forced out of the film industry ever came back.[5]

In terms of programming, the entertainment industry's recovery went much more slowly. Film studios and book publishers shied away from controversial material until the 1960s, when wider societal changes created a market for more daring movies and novels. Television and radio were even slower to cast off their post-McCarthy timidity. After all, they were dependent on advertising revenue for their survival, and companies that advertised their products during the 1950s and 1960s were terrified of offending any potential customers. Since that time, however, many artists, directors, musicians, writers, and playwrights actually seek out controversial subject matter—including McCarthyism itself. In 2005, in fact, George Clooney directed a film about Edward R. Murrow's famous McCarthy report called *Good Night, and Good Luck*. The film, which starred David Strathairn as Murrow, earned six Academy Award nominations.

American journalism also faced a long, slow road back to health after McCarthyism. Numerous news outlets had been manipulated by McCarthy and other Cold War demagogues into repeating reckless lies and distortions in exchange for increased profits. Their failure to examine these charges for truthfulness or question the motives of McCarthy and other Red-baiters was a shameful chapter in the history of American news reporting. Unfortunately, many modern critics of the news media in the United States argue that this lesson about McCarthyism has been forgotten—or was never learned in the first place. People surveying the state of American journalism in the twenty-first century often complain that many news organizations remain just as addicted to sensational headlines and superficial coverage as they were back in McCarthy's day.

The performance of the American press has been tainted by McCarthyism in another way as well. Even though McCarthy benefited enormously from media coverage of his every move, the senator frequently turned his fire on the press. He recognized that if he could cast doubt on the loyalty of American journalists, they would feel greater pressure to provide positive accounts of his anti-Communist crusade. "McCarthy set in motion the ideological forces that demonized the press, sowing doubts about the media's credibility and even its patriotism," wrote Pulitzer Prize–winning journalist Haynes Johnson. "McCarthy's message—that the American press was infested with biased liberals and, of course, Communists and Socialists—has been a source of national political divisiveness ever since."[6]

McCarthyism and the Abuse of State Power

Another aspect of McCarthyism that has reared its head repeatedly over the last half-century is governmental abuse of power. After McCarthy's fall, the anti-democratic and repressive tactics employed by congressional investigators, the FBI, and other governmental institutions during the Red Scare were widely condemned. Presidents, congressmen, cabinet officials, and agency administrators all promised that illegal surveillance of citizens and other unethical practices associated with McCarthyism would no longer be tolerated.

Unfortunately, these promises have not been kept. Once McCarthyism showed government officials how the power of the state could be used to punish political enemies and advance political goals, the temptation to make use of these weapons has often been too great for politicians and officials to resist. For example, Congress resisted calls to disband the House Un-American Activities Committee (HUAC), which was widely associated with McCarthyism. HUAC continued to conduct investigations (as the House Internal Security Committee) until 1975, when it was finally abolished.

During the 1960s and 1970s, the FBI operated a secret surveillance program called COINTELPRO (an acronym for Counterintelligence Program). This

This flyer was produced in the early 1960s by the National Committee to Abolish the Un-American Activities Committee, also known as HUAC.

program was designed to monitor, harass, disrupt, and "neutralize" domestic political organizations that did not meet with the approval of FBI director J. Edgar Hoover and White House officials. The program, which was carried out under both Democratic and Republican administrations, targeted a wide range of "subversives," including Communist and Socialist groups, the National Association for the Advancement of Colored People (NAACP) and other civil rights groups, anti-Vietnam War activists, organizations fighting for women's rights and Native American rights, and the white supremacist Ku Klux Klan.

COINTELPRO was officially terminated in 1971, after its existence came to light. But the U.S. Senate still launched a major investigation into the pro-

gram. The final report of the Select Committee to Study Governmental Operations with Respect to Intelligence Activities of the United States Senate
(commonly known as the Church Committee because it was chaired by
Democratic senator Frank Church of Idaho) found that the FBI program had
engaged in many of the same tactics that had been commonplace during
McCarthy's heyday:

> Many of the techniques used would be intolerable in a democ-
> ratic society even if all of the targets had been involved in vio-
> lent activity, but COINTELPRO went far beyond that.... The
> Bureau conducted a sophisticated vigilante operation aimed
> squarely at preventing the exercise of First Amendment rights
> of speech and association.... Groups and individuals have
> been harassed and disrupted because of their political views
> and their lifestyles. Investigations have been based upon vague
> standards whose breadth made excessive collection inevitable.
> Unsavory and vicious tactics have been employed—including
> anonymous attempts to break up marriages, disrupt meetings,
> ostracize persons from their professions, and provoke target
> groups into rivalries that might result in deaths.[7]

Other depressing examples of governmental corruption soon followed.
In 1974 President Richard M. Nixon—who had first achieved national prominence a quarter-century earlier for his role in the Alger Hiss spy case—was
forced to resign from office after revelations that his administration had
engaged in an assortment of illegal activities against its political enemies. In
the 1980s, the Reagan administration approved FBI surveillance of numerous
domestic organizations that were exercising their constitutional right to
oppose Reagan's anti-Communist policies in Central America. According to
critics like social activist Jamie Kalven, these "attacks of constitutional amne-
sia" seemed nearly inevitable whenever Americans felt "a heightened sense of
the nation's vulnerability in a dangerous world.... At such times, national
security concerns have eclipsed First Amendment values, yielding legislation,
administrative procedures, and judicial decisions that cut deeply into constitutional freedoms. Eventually, the fears and passions pass, but the laws and
precedents live on—a sort of shadow tradition, carrying forward past mistakes as future possibilities, available to be exploited during some later era of
tension and fear."[8]

McCarthyism in Twenty-First-Century America?

After the terrorist attacks on New York City and Washington, D.C., on September 11, 2001, President George W. Bush urged Congress to pass a variety of anti-terrorism measures. The most far-reaching of these measures was the USA Patriot Act. This legislation greatly broadened the authority of the FBI, the CIA, and other law enforcement agencies to carry out surveillance and other investigative techniques on American citizens so as to ward off future terrorist activity.

Public support for the proposed Patriot Act was very high, but it was not universally praised. Some Americans from both the political left and right criticized the bill as one that demanded too many sacrifices of basic constitutional rights. They expressed anxiety that the 2001 terrorist attacks (and subsequent U.S. military operations in Afghanistan and Iraq) might be laying the groundwork for a new age of McCarthyism in America. These concerns were heightened when Attorney General John Ashcroft and other defenders of the Patriot Act branded critics as unpatriotic: "To those who scare peace-loving people with phantoms of lost liberties," said Ashcroft, "your tactics aid terrorists."[9]

Bush signed the Patriot Act into law on October 26, 2001, after the bill passed both Houses of Congress with enthusiastic support from both Republicans and Democrats. Since its passage, civil liberties groups remain convinced that the Patriot Act empowers the government to commit serious violations of the constitutional rights of Americans without penalty. Defenders of the act remain equally convinced that the Act strikes an appropriate balance between national security and the preservation of constitutional rights. Emphasizing that the terrorists who attacked America in 2001 had plotted their violence while living in the United States, they continue to frame the Patriot Act as a sensible response to a dire threat. The truth, according to some observers, lies somewhere in between the arguments of the two camps. As the authors of a Patriot Act study in *Salon.com* put it, "both advocates and opponents are guilty of fear-mongering and distortion in some instances."[10]

Since the passage of the Patriot Act (and its renewal with minor changes in 2006), accusations of McCarthyite tactics have spread far beyond that single issue. During the first decade of the new century, in fact, Republicans and Democrats have routinely condemned each other for engaging in acts of

On October 26, 2001, President George W. Bush signed the Patriot Act into law. Hailed by its defenders as a necessary and appropriate response to the threat of terrorism, the Patriot Act has been faulted by critics for impinging on basic civil liberties.

"modern-day McCarthyism." Most of these fights have been different in one significant respect from the earlier controversies surrounding COINTELPRO, HUAC, Watergate, and the Patriot Act. Those clashes concerned alleged abuses of state power. The newest rounds of political warfare, though, have focused more on whether another element of McCarthyism—the character assassination or censorship of Americans who dare to hold opposing or unpopular views—is on the rise.

Republicans and some of their conservative constituencies have been accused of engaging in McCarthyism on a number of issues. Climate scientists have complained that skeptical Republicans and their allies have used intimidation and personal smears to suppress their warnings about the perils of global warming. Democrats and health reform advocates have charged Republicans with outrageous misrepresentations of the Affordable Care Act, a major health care reform law that was signed into law by President Barack Obama in early 2010. Republican criticisms of minority voting rights groups, Islamic organizations, liberal members of Congress, and other political opponents as "anti-American" have also sparked accusations that they are engaging in blatant McCarthyism for political gain. These charges reached new levels of intensity in March 2010, when a conservative political organization called Keep America Safe released a video questioning the loyalty and patriotism of officials in President Barack Obama's Justice Department (see "A Liberal Columnist Condemns the "al-Qaeda Seven" Video as Modern-Day McCarthyism," p. 195).

Conservative Republicans have flatly rejected most of these charges as weak attempts by Democrats to distract public attention from their own unpopular policy positions or questionable actions. In cases such as the "al-Qaeda Seven" controversy, many Republicans have defended their actions as perfectly reasonable (see "A Conservative Writer Defends the Legitimacy of Questions about the 'al-Qaeda Seven,'" p. 192). In some instances, they have even accused Democrats and progressive groups of engaging in McCarthyite tactics themselves. Republicans complain, for example, that the left has unfairly labeled conservatives as racists or homophobes. They also point to controversies such as the 2007 publication in the *New York Times* of an advertisement—paid for by the liberal anti-war political organization MoveOn.org—that accused U.S. general David Petraeus of "betraying" America by allegedly providing misleading reports about military operations in Iraq. The advertisement, which Republican John McCain described as "a McCarthyite attack on an American patriot," was swiftly denounced by Democrats and Republicans alike.[11]

Conservative Attempts to Rehabilitate McCarthy's Image

In recent years some conservative political activists and writers have sought to change the nation's longstanding view of McCarthy and his career. They insist that the McCarthy depicted in American history books of the past half-century is not the real McCarthy. They claim that the senator's record has been distorted and misunderstood, and that he actually con-

President Barack Obama in an appearance at a health care policy forum held in Washington, D.C., on August 8, 2009.

tributed to the improvement of national security in the 1950s by highlighting America's genuine problems with Communist spies. The most prominent of these attempts to present a more sympathetic portrait of McCarthy have included Arthur Herman's *Joseph McCarthy: Reexamining the Legacy of America's Most Hated Senator* (2000), Ann Coulter's *Treason: Liberal Treachery from the Cold War to the War on Terrorism* (2005), and M. Stanton Evans's *Blacklisted by History* (2007).

One of the main points of emphasis of conservative advocates for McCarthy is the Venona Project. This U.S. counterintelligence project decoded thousands of intercepted cables between spies in the United States and the Soviet Union from 1941 to 1946. Declassified by the U.S. government in the 1990s, the Venona Project confirmed that Communist spy activity was a significant security problem in the United States in the 1940s. Most historians also agree that the Venona documents greatly strengthened the body of evidence against accused spies like Julius Rosenberg and Alger Hiss.

But most historians reject the claim that the Venona Project documents exonerate McCarthy. As Venona Project scholar Harvey Klehr stated:

> Virtually none of the people that McCarthy claimed or alleged were Soviet agents turn up in Venona. He did identify a few small fry who we now know were spies but only a few. And there is little evidence that those he fingered were among the unidentified spies of Venona. Many of his claims were wildly inaccurate; his charges filled with errors of fact, misjudgments of organizations and innuendoes disguised as evidence. He failed to recognize or understand the differences among genuine liberals, fellow-traveling liberals, Communist dupes, Communists and spies—distinctions that were important to make. The new information from Russian and American archives does not vindicate McCarthy. He remains a demagogue, whose wild charges actually made the fight against Communist subversion more difficult.[12]

Such dismissals have not discouraged advocates for McCarthy from continuing their efforts to restore his reputation. Overall, though, most Americans still subscribe to the viewpoint that McCarthy was an unprincipled and power-hungry bully—and that the McCarthy era was a particularly ugly and fear-driven period in American history.

Notes

[1] Schrecker, Ellen. *Many Are the Crimes: McCarthyism in America.* Boston: Little, Brown, 1998, p. 360.

[2] Quoted in Quadagno, Jill. *One Nation Uninsured: Why the U.S. Has No National Health Insurance.* New York: Oxford University Press, 2005, p. 35.

[3] Quoted in Kearns, Doris. *Lyndon Johnson and the American Dream.* New York: Harper and Row, 1976, p. 252.

[4] Schrecker, p. 372.

[5] Ceplair, Larry, and Steven Englund. *The Inquisition in Hollywood: Politics in the Film Community, 1930-1960.* Urbana and Chicago: University of Illinois Press, 2003, pp. 418-22.

[6] Johnson, Haynes. *The Age of Anxiety: McCarthyism to Terrorism.* New York: Harcourt, 2005, p. 139.

[7] Select Committee to Study Governmental Operations with Respect to Intelligence Activities. Intelligence Activities and the Rights of Americans. *Final Report.* Washington, DC: Government Printing Office, 1976, p. 5.

[8] Kalven, Jamie. "At War with the First Amendment," *Bulletin of the Atomic Scientists,* January 1989, p. 57.

[9] Morgan, Ted. *Reds: McCarthyism in Twentieth-Century America.* New York: Random House, 2003, p. 599.

[10] Lithwich, Dahlia, and Julia Turner. "A Guide to the Patriot Act," *Salon.com,* September 8, 2003. Available online at http://www.slate.com/id/2087984/.

[11] Rhee, Foon. "Republicans Bash MoveOn.org over Anti-Petraeus Ad," *Boston Globe,* September 10, 2007, Available online at http://www.boston.com/news/politics/politicalintelligence/2007/09/romney _bashes_m.html.

[12] Klehr, Harvey. "Was Joe McCarthy Right?" Raleigh Spy Conference, November 11, 2005. Available online at http://www.raleighspyconference.com/news/news_11-07-05.aspx.

BIOGRAPHIES

Roy Cohn (1927-1986)
Lawyer and Chief Aide to Joseph McCarthy

Roy Marcus Cohn was born on February 20, 1927, in New York City. His father was Al Cohn, a state supreme court justice with strong ties to the Democratic Party. His mother was Dora Marcus, a wealthy heiress who reportedly spoiled her only son and taught him, as historian Geoffrey Ward wrote, that "rules applied to commoners, not royalty."

Cohn attended the finest private schools in New York City before enrolling at Columbia College, where he earned his bachelor's degree. He then entered Columbia Law School and earned a law degree in 1947 at age twenty. He had to wait a year to practice law in New York, which set a minimum age of twenty-one for admittance to the state bar. After joining the bar, however, his academic record and family connections translated into an offer to join the U.S. district attorney's office in New York City. During the next two years he helped secure convictions against a number of Americans accused of being Soviet spies.

Prosecutes Communists

In 1950 Cohn accepted a position as assistant U.S. attorney with the Justice Department in Washington, D.C. Almost immediately, Cohn became known throughout the nation's capital as one of the city's most aggressive and talented young lawyers—and as an unrelenting prosecutor of alleged Communists in the federal government. His work in the investigation and prosecution of Julius and Ethel Rosenberg, who were eventually executed for providing military secrets about the atomic bomb to the Soviet Union, brought him to the attention of Republican senator Joseph McCarthy. (Years later, Cohn claimed that he helped select the judge who would give the death sentence to the Rosenbergs, and that he had improper private discussions with the judge during the trial[1]).

Impressed by Cohn's hard-nosed manner and his clear hatred for Communists, McCarthy named him chief counsel to the Senate Permanent Investigations Subcommittee, which the Wisconsin politician had turned into a virtu-al one-man crusade against Reds lurking in American government and society. Cohn joined McCarthy in January 1953, and within a matter of weeks he had firmly established himself as the senator's right-hand man. Over the next year Cohn enthusiastically joined McCarthy in grilling suspected Communists and Communist sympathizers called before their committee. Their bullying tactics and careless accusations triggered rising opposition from the American public and fellow politicians. Still, their positions as two of Washington's most feared power brokers seemed secure until late 1953, when a simmering dispute between McCarthy-Cohn and the U.S. Army broke into public view.

The clash centered on G. David Schine, who McCarthy had previously added to his team at the request of Cohn. Schine and Cohn were close friends, and historians have long debated whether the two men were involved in a secret homosexual relationship. These rumors intensified after Cohn and Schine embarked on a controversial tour of State Department libraries in Europe in 1953 to seek out "subversive" materials and remove them from shelves.

Whatever the exact nature of the relationship between Cohn and Schine, historians agree that Cohn repeatedly sought special treatment from the U.S. Army for Schine, who was facing the draft. Army officials refused Cohn's repeated demands that Schine be made an officer and instead conscripted him as a private. They did give Schine preferential treatment once he entered the service, but Cohn remained furious about the whole matter. In the fall of 1953 McCarthy and Cohn retaliated by launching an investigation of alleged Com-munist agents and sympathizers in the army. But this offensive blew up in their faces when the army publicized their arm-twisting efforts on Schine's behalf.

In 1954 Senate investigators conducted the so-called Army-McCarthy Hearings to learn the truth about the whole dispute. By the time the hearings were over, McCarthy's career and reputation were in ruins. Cohn resigned his position under pressure and moved back to New York City, where he man-aged to carve out a career as a high-priced lawyer and power broker. He became known for representing a wide range of clients, from organized crime figures to celebrities from the worlds of music and film.

Controversial to the End

During the next three decades Cohn cultivated an image as a tough and ruthless lawyer who could use his political connections and wealth to "fix" the legal problems of most clients. He was repeatedly investigated for alleged professional misconduct. Cohn was accused of everything from tampering with witnesses and financial fraud to lying under oath, but he escaped conviction on these and other charges. Time after time, Cohn insisted that the criminal charges he faced were nothing more than harassment from political enemies.

Cohn also refused to apologize for any of the investigations that he and McCarthy had undertaken back in the early 1950s. He claimed that he felt no guilt about his actions during that time, and that he would do it all over again. Cohn also expressed no regrets about his numerous homophobic statements and anti-gay activities over the years, despite a strong body of evidence indicating that he was homosexual himself.

In the mid-1980s Cohn said that he was suffering from liver cancer. In reality, however, he had been diagnosed with AIDS in 1984. In the spring of 1986 Cohn's license to practice law was finally revoked by a panel of the New York State Bar Association. The panel determined that Cohn had engaged in a wide range of unethical and illegal conduct over a number of years. Cohn died of complications from AIDS on August 2, 1986.

Sources

Cohn, Roy, and Sidney Zion. *The Autobiography of Roy Cohn*. New York: St Martin's Press, 1988.

Oshinsky, David M. *A Conspiracy So Immense: The World of Joe McCarthy*. New York: Free Press, 1983.

Von Hoffman, Nicholas. *Citizen Cohn: The Life and Times of Roy Cohn*. New York: Doubleday, 1988.

Ward, Geoffrey. "Roy Cohn." *American Heritage,* July/Aug. 1988. Available online at http://www.americanheritage.com/articles/magazine/ah/1988/5/1988_5_12.shtml.

Notes

[1] Cohn, Roy, and Sidney Zion. *The Autobiography of Roy Cohn*. New York: St Martin's Press, 1988, pp. 60-66.

Martin Dies (1900-1972)
First Chairman of the House Un-American Activities Committee

Martin Dies Jr. was born in rural Mitchell County, Texas, on November 5, 1900. His father, Martin Dies Sr., was a lawyer and a Democratic member of the U.S. House of Representatives (from 1909 to 1919) who had been among Washington's most outspoken critics of America's open immigration policies. Young Dies followed in his father's footsteps professionally. After earning an undergraduate degree from the University of Texas in 1919, he earned a law degree from National University (now George Washington University) in Washington, D.C., in 1920. Dies then joined his father's law firm back in Texas, where he toiled for the next ten years.

Turns against Roosevelt's New Deal

In 1930 Dies ran for a seat in the U.S. Congress. After narrowly defeating the six-term incumbent in the Democratic primary, Dies easily won in the general election. He began a twelve-year stint in the U.S. House of Representatives on March 4, 1931; he was re-elected five consecutive times, from 1932 to 1940.

During Dies's first years in Congress, his position on various political issues closely matched those of the white farmers back in his district (poll taxes and other forms of repression effectively kept African Americans from exercising their right to vote in Texas and most other regions of the South during this era). Dies supported President Franklin D. Roosevelt's New Deal economic policies, which provided assistance to working-class Americans struggling to survive the Great Depression. But he also denounced blacks and immigrants as inferior, untrustworthy, and the source of many of America's economic and social problems. Dies, in fact, was an active supporter of the white supremacist Ku Klux Klan.

By 1935 Dies had become convinced that the United States's "problems" with Communism, labor radicals, and immigrants were all closely intertwined. He also believed that cultivating a strong "anti-radical" reputation might help him attain his goal of someday reaching the U.S. Senate. These factors led him to cut ties with the Roosevelt administration, which maintained a generally pro-labor and pro-immigrant outlook. By 1937 Dies was an outspoken critic of the New Deal, and in May of that year he used his standing as a member of the House Rules Committee to call for the formation of a special committee to investigate "un-American" activities in the United States.

Leads Early HUAC Investigations

Dies's resolution was supported by an anti–New Deal coalition of Republicans and conservative southern Democrats such as himself. On May 26, 1938, the House Special Committee on Un-American Activities was formed. Five years later the committee, which became known as the House Un-American Activities Committee (HUAC), was made a standing (permanent) committee by the House of Representatives.

Dies was designated the first chairman of HUAC, and he wasted no time in turning the committee into a weapon for crushing Communists and other "radicals" of the political left. In addition, Dies made effective use of the nation's newspaper and radio outlets to broadcast warnings about the evil Communists lurking in America's towns and institutions—and especially in the agencies carrying out Roosevelt's New Deal policies. "The Dies Committee pioneered the whole spectrum of slogans, techniques, and political mythologies that would later be called 'McCarthyism,'" wrote historian Robert Griffith. "It was the Dies Committee, for example, that popularized in the United States the technique of 'guilt by association,' through which a person is considered suspect because of the organizations to which he belongs or the friends whose company he keeps."[1] Despite some of its shameful excesses, however, the Dies Committee also did uncover a number of genuine cases where Communist agents *were* operating in the United States.

In 1940 Dies published *The Trojan Horse*, in which he warned that Communists and Nazis posed a dire threat to the future of the United States. That same year he established the Dies Foundation for Americanism, where he deposited his growing earnings from his anti-Communist writings and speeches.

Dies and HUAC faded from the public spotlight somewhat after the United States entered World War II in 1941, but Dies remained one of Washington's most powerful politicians. In April 1944, however, he was diagnosed with a possible case of throat cancer. This news, combined with the accumulated strain of years of political warfare with the Roosevelt administration, convinced Dies not to run for re-election that November.

After returning to Texas Dies discovered that he did not have throat cancer. He spent the next several years farming, but he also remained active in local and state politics. In 1952 he returned to the U.S. House of Representatives after winning an election for a new "at-large" seat in Texas. Upon returning to Washington after an eight-year absence, Dies found that he was unable to recapture his previous clout as an anti-Communist crusader. He could not even get his old seat back on the House Un-American Activities Committee. But he was warmly received by Senator Joseph McCarthy, who had become the nation's most famous Red-baiter. McCarthy declared that Dies would "go down in history as a heroic voice crying in the wilderness."[2]

Dies won re-election to the House two more times, but he failed in a 1957 bid for the U.S. Senate. He then retired from public life for good. Dies went back to Texas, where he became a regular columnist for *American Opinion*, the magazine of the right-wing John Birch Society, which is best-known for its anti-Communist orientation and its opposition to civil rights legislation. In 1966 he suffered a stroke. He died after suffering a second stroke on November 14, 1972, in Lufkin, Texas.

Sources

Griffith, Robert. *The Politics of Fear: Joseph R. McCarthy and the Senate.* Lexington: University Press of Kentucky, 1970; 2d ed., Amherst: University of Massachusetts Press, 1987.
Morgan, Ted. *Reds: McCarthyism in Twentieth-Century* America. New York: Random House, 2003.

Notes

[1] Griffith, Robert. *The Politics of Fear: Joseph R. McCarthy and the Senate.* Lexington: University Press of Kentucky, 1970; 2d ed., Amherst: University of Massachusetts Press, 1987, p. 32.
[2] Quoted in Morgan, Ted. *Reds: McCarthyism in Twentieth-Century America.* New York: Random House, 2003, p. 221.

Alger Hiss (1904-1996)
State Department Official Accused of Being a Soviet Agent

Alger Hiss was born on November 11, 1904, in Baltimore, Maryland. He was the fourth of five children born to Mary Livinia Hughes and Charles Alger Hiss, a business executive who committed suicide when young Alger was two years old. Hiss attended public schools in Baltimore, then enrolled at the city's prestigious Johns Hopkins University, where he earned a bachelor's degree in 1926. Later that year he entered Harvard Law School, where he received his law degree in 1929. Hiss then served a one-year term as law clerk to U.S. Supreme Court justice Oliver Wendell Holmes.

Serves as a Top Diplomat and Advisor

Hiss spent the next three years as an attorney with a leading law firm in Boston. In 1933 he joined the New Deal administration of President Franklin D. Roosevelt. He worked as an attorney in the departments of Agriculture, Justice, and State over the next several years. Hiss remained in the State Department throughout World War II, working as a top-level policy analyst and diplomat. In 1944 he was appointed to the Office of Special Political Affairs (OSPA), which was responsible for planning international recovery and diplomatic efforts that could be undertaken after the war. In the fall of 1944 he served as executive secretary at the Dumbarton Oaks Conference, a historic meeting of diplomats from the United States, China, the Soviet Union, and Great Britain. That gathering paved the way for the formation of the United Nations the following year.

Hiss also served as a key member of the U.S. delegation at the Yalta Conference of February 1945. By the time this summit was over, the leaders of the United States, the Soviet Union, and Great Britain had negotiated a wide-ranging agreement for establishment of the United Nations and post-war policies in Europe. A few months later, Hiss served as secretary-general of the

111

United Nations Conference on International Organization in San Francisco. This meeting, which ran from April through June, established the charter for the United Nations. In 1946 Hiss departed the State Department for the presidency of the Carnegie Endowment for International Peace, a private nonprofit organization devoted to promoting cooperation and communication among nations around the globe.

By the time Hiss took the helm of the Carnegie Endowment, he was well-known throughout Washington as a bright and talented foreign policy expert with ties to the nation's most influential progressive political circles. But within a year his seemingly secure existence was threatened by spectacular accusations that he was actually a Soviet spy with longstanding connections to American Communists.

Accused of Being a Communist Agent

Hiss's accuser was Whittaker Chambers, an ex-Communist who had become an editor for *Time* magazine. In August 1948 Chambers told the House Un-American Activities Committee (HUAC) that Hiss had been a fellow member of an underground Communist "cell" group back in the mid-1930s. Hiss not only denied the charges when HUAC called him to testify about the accusations, he also claimed that he had never even met Chambers before. Hiss also received public proclamations of support from a wide range of Democratic politicians and officials who dismissed the whole episode as contemptible Red-baiting.

Chambers, however, refused to back down. Instead he provided investigators with additional information to support his assertion that Hiss had once been an active agent for the Soviets, including convincing details about Hiss's personal life. As the HUAC investigation of Hiss intensified, the former State Department official changed his story. He acknowledged that he remembered Chambers as an acquaintance from the mid-1930s. Hiss testified, however, that he had known Chambers back then as George Crosley, a freelance writer to whom Hiss had rented an apartment and loaned a car. By this time, Representative Richard Nixon and other HUAC investigators were convinced that Hiss was lying about his past.

On December 15, 1948, Hiss was indicted on two charges of perjury—one for lying about his past knowledge of Chambers and one for lying about passing classified state secrets to Chambers. Hiss was not subject to spying charges because the statute of limitations on those crimes, which had allegedly taken place more than a decade earlier, had expired. Hiss maintained his innocence, and his perjury trial ended in a hung jury—one in which the jurors cannot reach unanimous agreement on a defendant's guilt or innocence. Prosecutors responded by calling a second trial. When the jurors returned from deliberations in this second trial on January 21, 1950, they announced a guilty verdict on both charges.

The verdict was met with disbelief by Hiss supporters like Secretary of State Dean Acheson, who reiterated his faith in Hiss's innocence. But Hiss's efforts to overturn the verdict on appeal failed, and he ended up serving forty-four months in Lewisburg Federal Prison. He was released on November 27, 1954.

Claims Innocence to the End

After his release from prison, Hiss relocated in Massachusetts and devoted the rest of his life to trying to prove his innocence. In 1957 he published *In the Court of Public Opinion,* in which he claimed that HUAC had falsified much of the evidence used against him. In 1975 the American Bar Association reinstated Hiss's license to practice law, which had been revoked upon his 1950 conviction. He thus became the first lawyer ever readmitted to the Massachusetts bar after a major criminal conviction. Thirteen years later he published an autobiography, *Recollections of a Life,* in which he once again insisted that he was innocent.

Hiss died on November 15, 1996, at the age of ninety-two in New York City. His passing brought a new flurry of articles and stories about the Hiss-Chambers case, which remains one of the most famous events of the McCarthy era. As the *New York Times* observed, "the case … became a source of obsessive fascination, a tangle of conspiracy theories and lingering doubts.… It was a kind of morality play that severed society along ideological and emotional lines. At Mr. Hiss's death, nearly 50 years after he was first publicly accused, followers of the case remained bitterly split over whether he was guilty, innocent or something in between."

Historians have split into different camps regarding Hiss as well. Some scholars believe that Hiss has been unfairly maligned over the years. They believe that he may have tried to hide old Communist ties, but that he did not work as a foreign agent. The consensus among most scholars, though, is that declassified secret documents from the Venona Project and other historical materials strongly indicate that Hiss did in fact carry out espionage activities for the Soviets during his years in the State Department. According to historians John Earl Haynes and Harvey Klehr, "The evidence from myriad sources—eyewitnesses and written documents, public testimony and private correspondence, fellow spies and Soviet intelligence officers, decrypted cables and long-closed archives—is overwhelming and conclusive"[1] that Hiss was a Soviet spy.

Sources

Hiss, Alger. *Recollections of a Life.* Boston: Little Brown, 1988.

Scott, Janny. "Alger Hiss, Divisive Icon of the Cold War, Dies at 92," *New York Times,* November 16, 1996.

Weinstein, Allen. *Perjury: The Hiss-Chambers Case.* 2nd rev. ed. New York: Knopf, 1997.

White, G. Edward. *Alger Hiss's Looking-Glass Wars: The Covert Life of a Soviet Spy.* New York: Oxford University Press, 2005.

Notes

[1] Haynes, John Earl, and Harvey Klehr. "Comment on Amy Knight's Review of *Spies* in the *Times Literary Supplement,*" 2009. Available online at http://www.johnearlhaynes.org/page73.html.

J. Edgar Hoover (1895-1972)
Director of the Federal Bureau of Investigation (FBI), 1924-1972

John Edgar Hoover was born in Washington, D.C., on January 1, 1895. His parents were Annie Marie (Scheitlin) Hoover and Dickerson Naylor Hoover, who worked for the U.S. Coast Guard. Bright and ambitious, young Hoover worked as a clerk at the Library of Congress to support himself in college. He graduated from George Washington University with a bachelor's degree in 1916, then added a law degree one year later.

A Rapid Rise to Power

In 1917 the United States entered World War I. Hoover was able to secure a position with the Department of Justice, which exempted him from the military draft. He spent the next two years working in the Justice Department's Bureau of Investigation, where he monitored German Americans and other immigrant "aliens" for potential security threats. In 1919 he was promoted by Attorney General A. Mitchell Palmer to head a new department known as the General Intelligence Division (GID), which was responsible for investigating radical groups in America. Hoover and his staff quickly identified thousands of "security risks," including Socialists, Communists, anarchists, labor organizers, social reformers, African-American leaders, and immigrants. Their findings became the basis for the controversial anti-Communist Palmer Raids of 1919 and 1920.

The Palmer Raids prompted a backlash from Americans anxious about violations of civil liberties, but Hoover himself managed to avoid being tainted. The whole affair, in fact, further burnished his reputation as a serious, loyal, and effective administrator. In June 1924 Attorney General Harlan Fiske Stone named Hoover interim director of the Bureau of Investigation (in 1935 the agency formally changed its name to the Federal Bureau of Investigation, or FBI). A few months later, the Wilson administration removed the interim tag from his title, and Hoover began his forty-eight-year directorship of the FBI in earnest.

Hoover quickly built the agency into a powerful force in American law enforcement and politics. He effectively lobbied Congress for higher funding to implement new training programs, establish new crime laboratories and investigative techniques (such as fingerprinting), and add more agents. At the same time, he reorganized the agency to make it more professional and disciplined. Finally, he shaped the bureau so that power and information was concentrated in his office. All of these trends made Hoover an enormously influential—and in many places feared—figure in Washington by the 1940s.

The reputations of both Hoover and the FBI soared during the 1930s and 1940s, when they became famous for bringing down notorious gangsters, solving bank robberies, and uncovering "radical" threats to American peace and tranquility. Hoover's reputation as a "law-and-order" man was further boosted by his continued condemnation of Communists and other subversives who, he insisted, remained intent on overthrowing the American way of life. "The communist movement in the Untied States began to manifest itself in 1919," he declared in 1947 testimony before the House Un-American Activities Committee. "Since then it has changed its name and its party line whenever expedient and tactical. But always it comes back to fundamentals ... and stands for the destruction of our American form of government; it stands for the destruction of American democracy; it stands for the destruction of free enterprise; and it stands for the creation of a 'Soviet of the United States.'"

An Ally of McCarthy

Hoover's fierce anti-Communist sentiments helped drive and shape the federal government's crackdown on alleged Communists, "fellow travelers," and sympathizers during the late 1940s and 1950s. Hoover moved decisively to place primary responsibility for the government's emerging campaign against Communism squarely with the FBI. Once he held the reins, he approved massive investigations that often ran roughshod over basic civil liberties. These investigations targeted thousands of Americans who might have been left untouched by a less conspiracy-minded director. As McCarthy scholar Ellen Schrecker explained, Hoover's FBI "subscribed to and pushed the oversimplified notion that all American Communists were Soviet puppets. It also tended to assume that there was little difference between party members, fellow travelers, and left-wing liberals. The FBI tended to lump together as Communists all the people who associated with the party and its many causes and to treat them all as if they endangered American security."

Hoover's outlook and his control of law enforcement resources made him a natural ally of Wisconsin senator Joseph McCarthy. When McCarthy carried out his notorious anti-Communist investigations of U.S. agencies, schools, and other institutions in the early 1950s, Hoover provided invaluable assistance to the senator. Hoover funneled all sorts of secret documents and investigative reports McCarthy's way. He also defended the senator against complaints that McCarthy was turning the legitimate pursuit of foreign agents into an erratic and wasteful "witch hunt."

In the summer of 1953, though, Hoover and McCarthy parted ways. Around that time Hoover sensed that the political winds were turning against the senator. He saw that tensions were rising between McCarthy and the administration of President Dwight D. Eisenhower, and he recognized that the dispute was eroding the senator's standing with his fellow Republicans. Hoover halted the transfer of FBI records to McCarthy, and he made sure that Eisenhower knew that the FBI director was on his side. The director's political instincts proved right; within a year's time the Army-McCarthy hearings had completely ruined McCarthy's career.

A Record of Civil Rights Violations

McCarthy's fall did not diminish Hoover's anti-Communist feelings, however. In 1956 he created a secret intelligence-gathering project called COINTELPRO, which the director used to carry out secret (and usually illegal) investigations of individuals and groups that he disliked. COINTELPRO targets during the 1950s and 1960s included a wide range of civil rights "agitators," including Martin Luther King Jr. In 1958 Hoover published *Masters of Deceit: The Story of Communism in America*. This book was actually ghostwritten by aides, but it conveyed Hoover's continued concern about the Red menace.

During the 1960s Hoover's lawbreaking escalated, as did his obsession with King. Convinced that the legendary civil rights activist was a dangerous Communist, he approved round-the-clock surveillance of King, as well as illegal wiretaps and other blatant violations of his civil liberties. Hoover also initiated a campaign of harassment of King that included threatening letters and other attempts at intimidation. But King refused to knuckle under to these abuses of police power, and Hoover never found the evidence of Communist influence that he was hoping for.

117

The existence of the FBI's secret COINTELPRO program was revealed to the American public in 1971. As people learned more and more about the program's complete disregard for civil liberties and individual rights, faith in Hoover and the FBI was badly shaken. But calls to replace Hoover received little support in Congress, in large part because many politicians feared that the director might have damaging information about them in his files. As it turned out, however, Hoover's nearly half-century reign over the FBI was nearly at an end. Hoover died of a heart attack in Washington, D.C., on May 2, 1972.

Sources

Gentry, Curt. *J. Edgar Hoover: The Man and the Secrets.* New York: W. W. Norton, 1991.

Powers, Richard Gid. *Secrecy and Power: The Life of J. Edgar Hoover.* New York: Free Press, 1993.

Theoharis, Athan G., and John Stuart Cox. *The Boss: J. Edgar Hoover and the Great American Inquisition.* Philadelphia: Temple University Press, 1988.

Notes

[1] Hoover, J. Edgar. Testimony before the House Committee on Un-American Activities. Hearings on H.R. 1884 and H.R. 2122, 80th Congress, 1st session, March 26, 1947.

[2] Schrecker, Ellen. *The Age of McCarthyism: A Brief History with Documents.* Boston: St. Martin's Press, 1994, p. 29.

Joseph McCarthy (1908-1957)
U.S. Senator and Namesake for the "Age of McCarthyism"

Joseph Raymond McCarthy was born on a farm outside of Grand Chute, Wisconsin, on November 15, 1908. His parents were Bridget (Tierney) McCarthy and Timothy McCarthy. The fifth of seven children, McCarthy left school at age fourteen to help out on the family farm. He then worked as a grocery store clerk and manager before returning to high school in 1929. McCarthy earned his high school diploma a mere nine months later. He then enrolled at Marquette University in Milwaukee in 1930. Paying his own way with a variety of part-time jobs, McCarthy earned his law degree from Marquette in 1935.

From Law to Politics

McCarthy opened a small law practice in Waupaca, Wisconsin, in 1935, but he soon joined a larger firm in Shawano (he became a partner in the practice in 1937). In 1936 McCarthy launched his first political campaign, for the position of Shawano district attorney. Running as a Democrat, he was defeated. Undaunted, McCarthy successfully ran for a circuit judge post in 1939. The thirty-year-old McCarthy thus became the youngest circuit judge ever elected in Wisconsin. Over the next few years McCarthy developed a reputation as a hard-working judge, although his impatient manner and inattention to some court rules raised eyebrows.

In July 1942 McCarthy took a leave of absence from his judgeship and enlisted in the U.S. Army, which was deploying forces all over the globe to fight Nazi Germany and its World War II allies. McCarthy's college education qualified him for an officer's commission, and after completing basic training he was made a first lieutenant in the Marines. He spent the remainder of the war stationed in the Pacific, where he participated in a dozen combat bombing missions as a tailgunner. McCarthy thus acquired a nickname—"Tailgunner Joe"—that he frequently highlighted in his later political career. McCarthy also received a number of military awards during his years as a Marine, but historians have determined that McCarthy falsified records and events to obtain some of these commendations.

McCarthy was still on active duty in 1944 when he unsuccessfully challenged incumbent Wisconsin senator Alexander Wiley for the Republican nomination to the U.S. Senate. In early 1945 McCarthy left the military with the rank of captain, and a few months later he was re-elected to his old position on the circuit court. He then began plotting a strategy to win election to the U.S. Senate in 1946.

The main obstacle in McCarthy's quest for the Senate seat was long-time incumbent Robert M. La Follette, a Progressive-turned-Republican whose father had been one of America's best-known politicians of the early twentieth century. Unseating La Follette was a tall order. But McCarthy campaigned tirelessly, and his relentless (and false) criticisms of La Follette as a draft dodger and war profiteer took a heavy toll on the incumbent. He also received the support of many conservative Republicans who disliked La Follette's moderate political positions. These factors enabled McCarthy to narrowly upset La Follette, then cruise to victory in the general election. McCarthy's victory made him the youngest member of the eightieth U.S. Congress, which was convened in January 1947.

A Meteoric Political Rise

During his first three years in the Senate, McCarthy's political future seemed shaky. Fellow Republicans applauded his victory over La Follette and his generally conservative voting record, and they echoed his frequent complaints that Democrats were too soft on Communism. But many senators disliked the hard-drinking, rough-mannered McCarthy personally. "Every time he took the [Senate] floor to speak, trouble seemed to follow," wrote biographer David Oshinsky. "Harried colleagues accused him of lying, manipulating figures, playing fast and loose with the Senate's most cherished traditions.... Most senators viewed him as a minor irritant, someone to be avoided whenever possible. It was only after McCarthy had hit the big time in 1950 that many would kick themselves for not dealing with him earlier, when it required neither great courage nor a full-scale public explanation."[1]

On February 9, 1950, however, McCarthy discovered a way to greatly increase his political power. He delivered a speech in Wheeling, West Virginia, in which he declared that he knew the identities of more than 200 Communists operating in the Truman administration's State Department. This accusation struck a nerve across America, which already harbored deep fears that a "fifth column" of secret Communist agents and sympathizers was undermining the United States from within. McCarthy's speech brought him more publicity than he had ever received before, and he took the lesson to heart. From that point on, the Wisconsin senator made the "Red Menace" the focal point of his career.

McCarthy's power and influence steadily rose over the next three years. Unfurling charges of disloyalty against high-ranking officials and low-level clerks alike, he became Washington's best-known investigator of Communist influence in the federal government. But his penchant for intimidation, distortion, and smear tactics also made him one of the most hated men in America. Critics condemned "McCarthyism" as a destructive force that was unleashing suspicion, division, and disregard for constitutional freedoms across the United States.

McCarthy's political clout became even greater in late 1953, when Republicans won control of the U.S. Senate. McCarthy's chairmanship of the Committee on Government Operations and its Permanent Subcommittee on Investigations (PSI) gave him even more leverage to pursue his political goals. But continued abuses of power by McCarthy and his chief aide, Roy Cohn, finally became too much for Republican president Dwight D. Eisenhower to ignore.

A Stunning Political Fall

In late 1953 Cohn and McCarthy improperly and repeatedly pressured the U.S. Army to give preferential treatment to G. David Schine, a former McCarthy aide. Around the same time the two men launched an investigation of potential Communist influence within the Army Signal Corps. As the investigation unfolded, McCarthy's poor treatment of Army general Ralph Zwicker infuriated the Eisenhower White House. The administration and the Army publicly charged that McCarthy's Signal Corps investigation was meant to punish the Army for its handling of the Schine affair.

Nationally televised hearings were held from April to June of 1954 to sort out the truth of the matter. These so-called Army-McCarthy hearings, which were overseen by the PSI under the temporary chairmanship of Senator Karl Mundt, destroyed McCarthy's career. The daily hearings revealed McCarthy's casual disregard for the truth, as well as his shady tactics. The final blow came on June 9, when the Army's chief counsel, Joseph Welch, turned to McCarthy and said, "Have you no sense of decency, sir, at long last?

Have you left no sense of decency?" To millions of Americans, Welch's remarks not only captured the essence of McCarthy's three-year campaign of Red-baiting, they also seemed to break the senator's spell over the nation.

After the hearings concluded, the U.S. Senate considered a variety of bills that condemned or censured McCarthy. They eventually settled on a formal resolution of condemnation that came up for a vote on December 2, 1954. It was approved by an overwhelming 67-22 margin. The resolution did not remove McCarthy from the Senate, but it made him nearly invisible. Widely ignored by colleagues and reporters alike, McCarthy's alcoholism worsened. In April 1957 he was hospitalized for liver problems associated with his heavy drinking. He died on May 2, 1957, of acute hepatitis. McCarthy was survived by his wife, Jean (Kerr) McCarthy, and an infant daughter that he and his wife had adopted five months earlier.

Sources

Herman, Arthur. *Joseph McCarthy: Reexamining the Life and Legacy of America's Most Hated Senator.* New York: Free Press, 1999.

Morgan, Ted. *Reds: McCarthyism in Twentieth-Century America.* New York: Random House, 2003.

Oshinsky, David M. *A Conspiracy So Immense: The World of Joe McCarthy.* New York: Free Press, 1983.

Reeves, Thomas C. *The Life and Times of Joe McCarthy: A Biography.* Lanham, MD: Madison Books, 1997.

Notes

[1] Oshinsky, David M. *A Conspiracy So Immense: The World of Joe McCarthy.* New York: Free Press, 1983, p. 54.

Arthur Miller (1915-2005)
Playwright and Author of The Crucible

Arthur Asher Miller was born on October 17, 1915, in New York City. His parents, Isidore and Gittel Miller, owned a small but successful women's clothing store and manufacturing business. The Millers lived in a comfortable neighborhood among fellow Jews until the 1929 onset of the Great Depression, which destroyed the family business and all of Miller's parents' life savings.

Crafting a Successful Life in the Theatre

The economic devastation forced Miller to work his way through college with a succession of clerical and warehouse jobs, but he still made a notable mark at the University of Michigan, where he enrolled in September 1934. In addition to his work and study obligations, Miller worked as a reporter and editor for the student newspaper. More importantly, he wrote his first plays (*No Villain* and *Honors at Dawn*) while at Michigan. Both of these works earned the young playwright scholarship awards from the university.

In 1938 Miller graduated from Michigan with a bachelor's degree in English. He promptly joined the Federal Theater Project (FTP), a New Deal effort to stage live plays and other artistic performances during the Depression. The program provided invaluable help to thousands of unemployed theater professionals, but funding for the project ended in 1939 after conservatives in Congress objected to the liberal perspective of many FTP productions.

During the 1940s Miller's reputation as a playwright steadily grew. Excused from World War II military service because of an old high school football injury, Miller crafted a series of dramas that took Broadway by storm. The first of his major successes was *All My Sons,* which earned him a 1946 Tony Award for best author. Three years later, his famous tragedy *Death of Salesman* opened on Broadway. The play was a huge commercial success, but it also earned Miller a second Tony Award as well as a Pulitzer Prize for Drama. It also received the prestigious New York Drama Circle Critics' Award.

Responding to McCarthyism with *The Crucible*

Miller's early successes in the theater coincided with a stark rise in fears about Communism across much of the United States. Millions of Americans became convinced during the 1940s and early 1950s that the Communist Soviet Union posed a mortal threat to the United States. Many of them also believed that thousands of treasonous "Reds" were lurking in the nation's schools, churches, unions, and government agencies. In many parts of the country, irresponsible and manipulative statements by lawmakers and newspapers had turned this fear into full-blown hysteria. During this period, many Americans urged their fellow citizens not to turn on each other or permit basic constitutional rights to be trampled. But their voices were drowned out by those of investigators like Wisconsin senator Joseph McCarthy, who insisted that America was riddled with subversives.

Miller watched the unfolding of "McCarthyism" across America with mounting alarm:

> It was not only the rise of "McCarthyism" that moved me, but something which seemed much more weird and mysterious. It was the fact that a political, objective, knowledgeable campaign from the far Right was capable of creating not only a terror, but a new subjective reality.... It was as though the whole country had been born anew, without a memory even of certain elemental decencies which a year or two earlier no one would have imagined could be altered, let alone forgotten. Astounded, I watched men pass me by without a nod whom I had known rather well for years; and again, the astonishment was produced by my knowledge, which I could not give up, that the terror in these people was being knowingly planned and consciously engineered, and yet that all they knew was terror.[1]

In 1952 Miller decided to write a play about McCarthyism and its impact on American life. But Miller did not compose a play featuring McCarthy, leaders of the House Un-American Activities Committee, and other Red-baiters of the era. The playwright instead wrote about the infamous Salem, Massachusetts, witch trials of 1692-1693, in which twenty townspeople were executed after they were falsely accused of practicing witchcraft. Miller's play, which he called *The Crucible*, opened at the Beck Theatre in New York's Broadway district on January 22, 1953. *The Crucible* received mixed reviews when it first opened, although it also won a "Best Play" Tony Award. As time passed, however, more and more Americans praised the allegorical drama's clear condemnation of McCarthyism and mob rule. Miller, meanwhile, was hailed as a brave truth teller at a time when many American politicians, artists, and writers feared to cross McCarthy.

HUAC responded to the play by opening an investigation on Miller. He was subpoenaed to testify before the committee in both 1956 and 1957. During this time, investigators repeatedly questioned him about his relationships with known Communists and liberal activists. Miller freely answered questions about his liberal political leanings. He also acknowledged that in the 1940s he signed a number of appeals and protest letters crafted by Communist groups, including statements criticizing HUAC and the Smith Act. But Miller refused to answer their demands that he identify fellow writers and playwrights who might harbor Communist sympathies or beliefs. A judge subsequently found Miller guilty of contempt of Congress and sentenced him to thirty days in prison, revocation of his passport, and a $500 fine. In 1958, however, the U.S. Court of Appeals overturned his conviction.

One of America's Most Famous Dramatists

During the late 1950s and 1960s Miller's personal life overshadowed his professional accomplishments in other ways as well. In 1956 he divorced his first wife, Mary Slattery, to marry the glamorous film star Marilyn Monroe. Their tumultuous marriage ended in divorce in 1961, and in August 1962 Monroe died of an apparent drug overdose. Miller, meanwhile, married photographer Inge Morath on February 17, 1962. They had two children, and they remained married until her death in 2002.

Miller's reputation as one of America's most celebrated playwrights is unquestioned, however. *The Crucible* and *Death of a Salesman* stand as his most famous works, but he wrote more than thirty stage plays and nonfiction works during his lifetime, many of which garnered critical praise and awards. Miller also received some of the world's leading individual honors for artists, including the National Medal of Arts (1993), the Dorothy and Lillian Gish Prize (1999), and the 2002 Principe de Asturias Prize for Literature as "the undisputed master of modern drama." In 1996 a film adaptation of *The Crucible,* starring

Daniel Day-Lewis, was warmly received by critics and audiences alike. Miller died of heart failure after a long period of poor health on February 10, 2005.

Sources

Gottfried, Martin. *Arthur Miller: His Life and Work.* Cambridge, MA: Da Capo Press, 2004.
Miller, Arthur. *The Theater Essays of Arthur Miller.* Edited by Robert A. Martin and Steven R. Centola. Revised and expanded ed. Cambridge, MA: Da Capo Press, 1996.

Notes

[1] Miller, Arthur. *The Theater Essays of Arthur Miller.* Edited by Robert A. Martin and Steven R. Centola. Revised and expanded ed. Cambridge, MA: Da Capo Press, 1996, pp. xxxi-xxxii.

Edward R. Murrow (1908-1965)
Radio and Television Journalist

Egbert Roscoe Murrow was born in Greensboro, North Carolina, on April 25, 1908. His parents were Roscoe Murrow and Ethel (Lamb) Murrow. He spent most of his youth in northern Washington State, where he was an excellent student and debater. After graduating from high school he attended Stanford University and then Washington State College (now Washington State University). In 1929 he was elected president of the National Student Federation of America. After earning a bachelor's degree in speech from Washington State in 1930, Murrow moved to New York City with the goal of launching a career in journalism.

Gains Fame as World War II Reporter

In 1932 Murrow accepted a position as assistant director of the Institute of International Education. Three years later, he accepted a position with the CBS radio network as director of talks and education. This move to CBS marked the beginning of a thirty-year affiliation with the broadcast network. In 1937 CBS appointed him director of its European Bureau in London. The position was an administrative one and did not involve actual on-air reporting, but within a year Murrow was regularly delivering news stories over the air from all around Europe.

Many of Murrow's early journalistic efforts focused on aggression by Nazi Germany against its European neighbors. He remained in England when World War II broke out in September 1939. One year later, he delivered live radio broadcasts from London throughout the deadly German bombing raids of that city and other population centers. By the time the German bombing "blitz" ended the following spring, Murrow's nightly reports had made him a famous journalist on both sides of the Atlantic. As the war progressed, Murrow also hired and trained a stable of other correspondents who provided excellent, hard-hitting coverage. These correspondents, including Eric Sevareid, Howard K. Smith, Mary Marvin Breckinridge, Cecil Brown, Charles

Collingwood, and Richard C. Hottelet, became known throughout the news industry as "Murrow's Boys."

After the war ended in 1945 Murrow returned to America. He briefly served as director of public affairs for CBS, but in 1947 he decided to return to journalism. He spent the next two years as a reporter and anchor for the *CBS Evening News*. In 1950 he began a two-year stint as host of the radio news show *Hear It Now*. In 1951 CBS decided to take the program to television as *See It Now*, with Murrow as host and co-producer (with Fred W. Friendly). Murrow also took on other responsibilities over the next several years, including a popular program of celebrity interviews called *Person to Person*, which he hosted from 1953 to 1959. But it was the public affairs program *See It Now* for which Murrow remained best-known—especially after he used the show as a vehicle to condemn Wisconsin senator Joseph McCarthy and his Red-baiting tactics.

Stands Up to McCarthy

Murrow and Friendly broadcast many notable episodes of *See It Now* during its run from 1951 to 1958. The program, which was a half-hour in length until 1955, when it expanded to an hour and aired less frequently, was known as the best news program of its time. But none of its broadcasts became as famous as the one that appeared in America's living rooms on March 9, 1954. That entire show was devoted to examining the anti-Communist crusading of McCarthy.

McCarthy's political power, flair for dramatic speeches, and willingness to tar opponents as evil Communists had transformed him into the most feared man in America in the early 1950s. By 1954, however, his reckless Red-baiting and abusive manner had become a source of frustration and embarrassment even to some staunch anti-Communists. The decision by Murrow and Friendly to hold McCarthy's methods and honesty up to scrutiny thus came at a very bad time for the senator. In addition, Murrow's decision to close the show by appealing to Americans to reject McCarthyism was influential with many viewers who had followed the journalist since his World War II days. By the end of 1954 the public backlash to which Murrow contributed had crushed McCarthy and left him politically powerless.

In some respects the McCarthy program was Murrow's last great moment in the public spotlight. He continued to host *See It Now* for another four years, but his relations with executives at CBS became strained. The situation worsened in 1958, when he delivered a harsh speech to the Radio and Television News Directors Association (RTNDA) blaming industry executives for creating a medium that was being used to "detract, delude, amuse, and insulate" the public rather than educate them. Murrow made contributions to several CBS news specials in 1959 and 1960, but in 1961 he left CBS to accept an offer from President John F. Kennedy to head the U.S. Information Agency (USIA). He remained there until 1964, when health problems forced him to resign. A lifelong smoker, Murrow died of cancer in New York on April 27, 1965.

Murrow received numerous journalistic honors during his lifetime, including nine Emmy Awards, two Polk Awards, and seven Peabody Awards. He also received the nation's highest civilian honor, the Presidential Medal of Freedom, in 1964. Today, Murrow is still remembered as "the most distinguished and renowned figure in the history of American broadcast journalism. He was a seminal force in the creation and development of electronic newsgathering as both a craft and a profession.... More than anyone else, he invented the traditions of television news."[1]

Sources

Kendrick, Alexander. *Prime-Time: The Life of Edward R. Murrow*. Boston: Little, Brown, 1969.

Sperber, A. M. *Murrow, His Life and Times*. New York: Freundlich, 1986.

Notes

[1] "Edward R. Murrow, Broadcast Journalist." Museum of Broadcast Communications. Available online at http://www.museum.tv/eotvsection.php?entrycode=murrowedwar.

Joseph Welch (1890-1960)
Chief Counsel for the Army during the Army-McCarthy Hearings

Joseph Nye Welch was born in Primghar, Iowa, on October 22, 1890. He was the youngest of seven children in a farming family. His father was a former merchant seaman, while his mother had been an indentured servant from Great Britain. He attended Iowa's Grinnell College, where he graduated Phi Beta Kappa in 1914. Welch then entered Harvard Law School, earning his law degree in 1917. That same year he married Judith Lydon, with whom he eventually had two children.

Launches a Distinguished Law Career

Welch trained as an officer during World War I, which ended in 1919. He then resumed his fledgling law career, taking a position with the Boston law firm of Hale and Dorr in 1919. Welch thrived there, and in 1923 he was made a partner. In 1936 Welch was promoted to senior partner, and he oversaw much of the firm's civil law and trial work in that capacity.

During the late 1940s and early 1950s Welch became increasingly anxious about the spread of McCarthyism in America. He was a registered Republican, but he disapproved of the Red-baiting tactics used by some conservative politicians in Washington. Welch also was a strong believer in civil liberties, and on several occasions he volunteered his legal expertise without pay to Massachusetts defendants who were accused of being radicals and subversives.

Faces Off with McCarthy

In early 1954 Welch was approached by top U.S. military officials to serve as lead counsel in an upcoming legal confrontation with Joseph McCarthy, the anti-Communist senator who had become the unquestioned leader of America's mid-century Red-hunting crusade—or witch hunt, according to critics. The dispute centered on whether McCarthy and his chief aide, Roy Cohn, had pressured the army to give preferential treatment to Private G. David Schine, who had once been a member of McCarthy's staff. Welch agreed to represent the army without financial compensation in the case, which was being heard by the U.S. Senate's Permanent Subcommittee on Investigations (PSI).

The so-called Army-McCarthy hearings, which were broadcast live on national television, convened on April 22, 1954, and closed on June 17, 1954. As the hearings unfolded, Welch consistently cultivated a friendly, courteous, and low-key manner. The American public responded very favorably to Welch's "old-fashioned" ways. By contrast, the arrogance and belligerence displayed day after day by McCarthy and Cohn did not help their cause in the court of public opinion.

Still, the pivotal moment in the case came when Welch set aside his folksy and agreeable demeanor to issue a stern rebuke to McCarthy over his relentless Red-baiting. The scolding came on June 9, after McCarthy accused a young associate in Welch's law firm of being a former member of a lawyer's guild that the senator claimed was actually a Communist "front" group. Welch responded to the accusation with quiet outrage, delivering an eloquent defense of the young lawyer. He then concluded his remarks with a devastating query to McCarthy: "Have you no sense of decency, sir, at long last? Have you left no sense of decency?"[1]

Welch's condemnation of McCarthy was applauded across the country. Journalist Mary McGrory spoke for millions of Americans when she wrote that "Mr. Welch came to Washington to defend the army. But he had his finest hour defending a friend."[2] McCarthy never recovered from this dramatic exchange with Welch. By the time the hearings concluded eight days later, the senator's career lay in ruins. The U.S. Senate voted to condemn McCarthy's behavior before the year was out.

The Army-McCarthy hearings had the opposite effect on Welch. After the hearings concluded, Welch was invited to the White House, where Republican president Dwight D. Eisenhower—who hated McCarthy—warmly congratulated him on a job well done. He was also the subject of numerous glowing stories in the press and on television. In 1956 Welch served as narrator of a critically acclaimed television series on the U.S. Constitution, and in 1959 he portrayed the trial judge in the film *Anatomy of a Murder*. Welch died on October 6, 1960, in Hyannis, Massachusetts.

Sources

Oshinsky, David M. *A Conspiracy So Immense: The World of Joe McCarthy*. New York: Free Press, 1983.
Shogan, Robert. *No Sense of Decency: The Army-McCarthy Hearings*. Chicago: Ivan R. Dee, 2009.

Notes

[1] "McCarthy Hearings, 1954." U.S. Senate Historical Office. Available online at www.senate.gov/art andhistory/history/common/generic/News McCarthy Hearings.htm.

[2] McGrory, Mary. "Mr. Welch Defends One Friend and Finds He's Made Many." In *The Best of Mary McGrory: A Half-Century of Washington Commentary.* Edited by Phil Gailey. Kansas City, MO: Andrews McMeel, 2006, p. 1.

PRIMARY SOURCES

The Smith Act Takes Aim at American Communists

Anxieties about the alleged threat to national security posed by Communists and Nazis led Congress to pass the Alien Registration Act. Better known as the Smith Act, in tribute to one of its key architects, Democratic representative Howard W. Smith of Virginia, the legislation was approved overwhelmingly in Congress on June 28, 1940, and signed by President Franklin D. Roosevelt. The act, which is excerpted below, was actively enforced until 1957, when the U.S. Supreme Court overturned many convictions under the act as unconstitutional.

AN ACT

To prohibit certain subversive activities; to amend certain provisions of law with respect to the admission and deportation of aliens; to require the fingerprinting and registration of aliens; and for other purposes.

Be it enacted by the Senate and House of Representatives of the United States of America in Congress assembled,

TITLE I

Section 1. (a) It shall be unlawful for any person, with intent to interfere with, impair, or influence the loyalty, morale, or discipline of the military or naval forces of the United States—

(1) to advise, counsel, urge, or in any manner cause insubordination, disloyalty, mutiny, or refusal of duty by any member of the military or naval forces of the United States; or

(2) to distribute any written or printed matter which advises, counsels, or urges insubordination, disloyalty, mutiny, or refusal of duty by any member of the military or naval forces of the United States.

(b) For the purposes of this section, the term "military or naval forces of the United States" includes the Army of the United States, as defined in section 1 of the National Defense Act of June 3, 1916, as amended (48 Stat. 153; U.S.C., title 10, sec. 2), the Navy, Marine Corps, Coast Guard, Naval Reserve, and Marine Corps Reserve of the United States; and, when any merchant vessel is commissioned in the Navy or is in the service of the Army or the Navy, includes the master, officers, and crew of such vessel.

Sec. 2. (a) It shall be unlawful for any person—

(1) to knowingly or willfully advocate, abet, advise, or teach the duty, necessity, desirability, or propriety of overthrowing or destroying any government in the United States by force or violence, or by the assassination of any officer of any such government;

(2) with the intent to cause the overthrow or destruction of any government in the United States, to print, publish, edit, issue, circulate, sell, distribute, or publicly display any written or printed matter advocating, advising, or teaching the duty, necessity, desirability, or propriety of overthrowing or destroying any government in the United States by force or violence.

(3) to organize or help to organize any society, group, or assembly of persons who teach, advocate, or encourage the overthrow or destruction of any government in the United States by force or violence; or to be or become a member of, or affiliate with, any such society, group, or assembly of persons, knowing the purposes thereof.

(b) For the purposes of this section, the term "government in the United States" means the Government of the United States, the government of any State, Territory, or possession of the United States, the government of the District of Columbia, or the government of any political subdivision of any of them.

Sec. 3. It shall be unlawful for any person to attempt to commit, or to conspire to commit, any of the acts prohibited by the provisions of this title.

Sec. 4. Any written or printed matter of the character described in section 1 or section 2 of this Act, which is intended for use in violation of this Act, may be taken from any house or other place in which it may be found, or from any person in whose possession it may be, under a search warrant issued pursuant to the provisions of title XI of the Act entitled "An Act to punish acts of interference with the foreign relations, the neutrality and the foreign commerce of the United States, to punish espionage, and better to enforce the criminal laws of the United States, and for other purposes", approved June 15, 1917 (40 Stat. 228; U.S.C., title 18, ch. 18).

Sec. 5. (a) Any person who violates any of the provisions of this title shall, upon conviction thereof, be fined not more than $10,000 or imprisoned for not more than ten years, or both.

(b) No person convicted of violating any of the provisions of this title shall, during the five years next following his conviction, be eligible for employment by the United States, or by any department or agency thereof (including any corporation the Stock of which is wholly owned by the United States)....

Source: Alien Registration Act of 1940, Public Law 670, *U.S. Statutes at Large,* 54 (1940), 76th Congress, 3rd Session, pp. 670-676.

Hollywood Studios Issue "The Waldorf Statement"

Hollywood was hard hit by the intensifying search for Communist agents in post-war America. Hearings called by the House Un-American Activities Committee (HUAC) to investigate Reds in Hollywood garnered massive headlines, as did the defiance of the so-called Hollywood Ten, a group of writers and directors who were blacklisted by the film industry for their stance toward HUAC. Desperate to show both Congress and the American public that they were loyal to America, the major Hollywood film studios got together and issued the "Waldorf Statement" on December 3, 1947. The "Waldorf Statement," reprinted here, is regarded by historians as the beginning of the blacklisting period in the entertainment industry.

Members of the Association of Motion Picture Producers deplore the action of the ten Hollywood men who have been cited for contempt. We do not desire to prejudge their legal rights, but their actions have been a disservice to their employers and have impaired their usefulness to the industry.

We will forthwith discharge or suspend without compensation those in our employ and we will not re-employ any of the ten until such time as he is acquitted or has purged himself of contempt and declares under oath that he is not a Communist.

On the broader issues of alleged subversive and disloyal elements in Hollywood, our members are likewise prepared to take positive action.

We will not knowingly employ a Communist or a member of any party or group which advocates the overthrow of the Government of the United States by force or by illegal or unconstitutional methods. In pursuing this policy, we are not going to be swayed by hysteria or intimidation from any source. We are frank to recognize that such a policy involves dangers and risks. There is the danger of hurting innocent people. There is the risk of creating an atmosphere of fear. Creative work at its best cannot be carried on in an atmosphere of fear. We will guard against this danger, this risk, this fear. To this end we will invite the Hollywood talent guilds to work with us to eliminate any subversives, to protect the innocent, and to safeguard free speech and a free screen wherever threatened.

Source: Motion Picture Association of America, The Waldorf Statement, issued December 3, 1947. Reprinted in Ceplair, Larry, and Steven Englund. *The Inquisition in Hollywood: Politics in the Film Community, 1930-1960.* Garden City, NY: Anchor Press/ Doubleday, 1980, p. 445.

A Communist Screenwriter Defies the House Un-American Activities Committee

Most Americans who were called to testify before the House Un-American Activities Committee (HUAC) were eager to please. Others refused to answer questions, citing Fifth Amendment protections, but still tried to avoid antagonizing their interrogators. A few memorable witnesses, however, were openly combative. One such witness was John Howard Lawson, who appeared before HUAC on October 27, 1947. Lawson was a dedicated Communist and prominent member of the Screen Actors Guild. His clashes with HUAC and its chairman, Representative J. Parnell Thomas, turned him into a member of the so-called Hollywood Ten, a group of writers and directors who were blacklisted by the film industry. Lawson was eventually found guilty of contempt of Congress, for which he received a one-year prison sentence and a $1,000 fine.

Lawson: Chairman, I have a statement here which I wish to make—

Chairman: Well, all right, let me see your statement.

(Statement handed to the chairman.)

Chairman: I don't care to read any more of the statement. The statement will not be read. I read the first line.

Lawson: You have spent one week vilifying me before the American public—

Chairman: Just a minute—

Lawson: And you refuse to allow me to make a statement on my rights as an American citizen.

Chairman: I refuse you to make the statement, because of the first sentence in your statement. That statement is not pertinent to the inquiry.

Now, this is a congressional committee—a congressional committee set up by law. We must have orderly procedure, and we are going to have orderly procedure.

Mr. Stripling, identify the witness.

Lawson: The rights of American citizens are important in this room here, and I intend to stand up for those rights, Congressman Thomas.

Chief Investigator Robert E. Stripling: Mr. Lawson, will you state your full name, please?

139

Lawson: I wish to protest against the unwillingness of this committee to read a statement, when you permitted Mr. Warner, Mr. Mayer, and others to read statements in this room.

My name is John Howard Lawson....

Stripling: What is your occupation, Mr. Lawson?

Lawson: I am a writer.

Stripling: How long have you been a writer?

Lawson: All my life—at least 35 years—my adult life.

Stripling: Are you a member of the Screen Writers Guild?

Lawson: The raising of any question here in regard to membership, political beliefs, or affiliation—

Stripling: Mr. Chairman—

Lawson: Is absolutely beyond the powers of this committee.

Stripling: Mr. Chairman—

Lawson: But—

(The chairman pounding gavel.)

Lawson: It is a matter of public record that I am a member of the Screen Writers Guild.

Stripling: I ask—

[Applause.]

Chairman: I want to caution the people in the audience: You are the guests of this committee and you will have to maintain order at all times. I do not care for any applause or any demonstrations of one kind or another.

Stripling: Now, Mr. Chairman, I am also going to request that you instruct the witness to be responsive to the questions.

Chairman: I think the witness will be more responsive to the questions.

Lawson: Mr. Chairman, you permitted—

Chairman (pounding gavel): Never mind—

Lawson (continuing): Witnesses in this room to make answers of three or four or five hundred words to questions here.

Chairman: Mr. Lawson, you will please be responsive to these questions and not continue to try to disrupt these hearings.

Lawson: I am not on trial here, Mr. Chairman. This committee is on trial here before the American people. Let us get that straight.

Chairman: We don't want you to be on trial.

Stripling: Mr. Lawson, how long have you been a member of the Screen Writers Guild?

Lawson: Since it was founded in its present form, in 1933.

Stripling: Have you ever held any office in the guild?

Lawson: The question of whether I have held office is also a question which is beyond the purview of this committee.

(The chairman pounding gavel.)

Lawson: It is an invasion of the right of association under the Bill of Rights of this country.

Chairman: Please be responsive to the question.

Lawson: It is also a matter—

(The chairman pounding gavel.)

Lawson: Of public record—

Chairman: You asked to be heard. Through your attorney, you asked to be heard, and we want you to be heard. And if you don't care to be heard, then we will excuse you and we will put the record in without your answers.

Lawson: I wish to frame my own answers to your questions, Mr. Chairman, and I intend to do so....

It is absolutely beyond the power of this committee to inquire into my association in any organization.

Chairman: Mr. Lawson, you will have to stop or you will leave the witness stand. And you will leave the witness stand because you are in contempt. That is why you will leave the witness stand. And if you are just trying to force me to put you in contempt, you won't have to try much harder. You know what has happened to a lot of people that have been in contempt of this committee this year, don't you?

Lawson: I am glad you have made it perfectly clear that you are going to threaten and intimidate the witnesses, Mr. Chairman.

(The chairman pounding gavel.)

Lawson: I am an American and I am not at all easy to intimidate, and don't think I am.

(The chairman pounding gavel.) ...

Chairman: (pounding gavel). Mr. Lawson, just quiet down again.

Mr. Lawson, the most pertinent question that we can ask is whether or not you have ever been a member of the Communist Party. Now, do you care to answer that question?

Lawson: You are using the old technique, which was used in Hitler Germany in order to create a scare here—

Chairman (pounding gavel): Oh—

Lawson: In order to create an entirely false atmosphere in which this hearing is conducted—

(The chairman pounding gavel) ...

Chairman: Stand away from the stand—

Lawson: I have written Americanism for many years, and I shall continue to fight for the Bill of Rights, which you are trying to destroy.

Chairman: Officers, take this man away from the stand—

[Applause and boos.]

Chairman (pounding gavel): There will be no demonstrations. No demonstrations, for or against. Everyone will please be seated....

Source: Lawson, John Howard, testimony of October 27, 1947. House Committee on Un-American Activities. *Hearings Regarding the Communist Infiltration of the Motion Picture Industry,* 80th Congress, 1st Session, October 1947. Washington, DC: Government Printing Office, 1947.

Whittaker Chambers and Alger Hiss Testify before HUAC

The downfall of Alger Hiss, a former high-ranking official in the State Department, came at the hands of Whittaker Chambers. An ex-Communist, Chambers told the House Un-American Activities Committee (HUAC) that he and Hiss had been members of the same underground Communist cell group in the mid-1930s. When Hiss denied the charges, HUAC intensified its efforts to find out which of the two men was lying.

The first excerpt below is from Chambers's testimony at a private HUAC hearing conducted in New York City on August 7, 1948. This hearing was chaired by Richard M. Nixon, a Republican representative from California who would later go on to become America's thirty-seventh president. Nine days later, Hiss testified at another HUAC hearing held in Washington, D.C. During his testimony, featured in the second excerpt below, Hiss confirmed many details of his personal life that Chambers had mentioned, from the breed of dog Hiss once owned to his excitement over a long-ago sighting of a rare bird. From this point forward, HUAC members were convinced that Hiss was lying about his past.

Testimony of Whittaker Chambers, August 7, 1948

Nixon: Do you solemnly swear the testimony you are about to give will be the truth, the whole truth, and nothing but the truth, so help you God?

Chambers: I do.

Nixon: Be seated. Mr. Chambers, you are aware of the fact that Mr. Alger Hiss appeared before this committee, before the Un-American Activities Committee, in public session and swore that the testimony which had been given by you under oath before this committee was false. The committee is now interested in questioning you further concerning your alleged acquaintanceship with Mr. Alger Hiss so that we can determine what course of action should be followed in this matter in the future.

Mr. Hiss in his testimony was asked on several occasions whether or not he had ever known or knew a man by the name of Whittaker Chambers. In each instance he categorically said "No."

At what period did you know Mr. Hiss? What time?

Chambers: I knew Hiss, roughly, between the years 1935 to 1937.

Nixon: Do you know him as Mr. Alger Hiss?

Chambers: Yes.

Nixon: Did you happen to see Hiss' pictures in the newspapers as a result of these recent hearings?

Chambers: Yes; I did.

Nixon: Was that the man you knew as Alger Hiss?

Chambers: Yes; that is the man.

Nixon: You are certain of that?

Chambers: I am completely certain.

Nixon: During the time that you knew Hiss, did he know you as Whittaker Chambers?

Chambers: No, he did not.

Nixon: By what name did he know you?

Chambers: He knew me by the party name of Carl.

Nixon: Did he ever question the fact that he did not know your last name?

Chambers: Not to me.

Nixon: Why not?

Chambers: Because in the underground Communist Party the principle of organization is that functionaries and heads of the group, in other words, shall not be known by their right names but by pseudonyms or party names....

Nixon: I understood you to say that Mr. Hiss was a member of the party.

Chambers: Mr. Hiss was a member of the Communist Party.

Nixon: How do you know that?

Chambers: I was told by Mr. [J.] Peters.

Nixon: You were told that by Mr. Peters?

Chambers: Yes.

Nixon: On what facts did Mr. Peters give you?

Chambers: Mr. Peters was the head of the entire underground, as far as I know.

Nixon: The entire underground of the Communist Party?

Chambers: Of the Communist Party in the United States.

Nixon: Do you have any other evidence, any factual evidence, to bear out your claim that Mr. Hiss was a member of the Communist Party?

Chambers: Nothing beyond the fact that he submitted himself for the 2 or 3 years that I knew him as a dedicated and disciplined Communist.

Nixon: Did you obtain his party dues from him?

Chambers: Yes, I did.

Nixon: Over what period of time?

Chambers: Two or three years, as long as I knew him....

[*Nixon then shifts the questioning to details of Hiss's personal life.*]

Nixon: What name did Mrs. Hiss use in addressing Mr. Hiss?

Chambers: Usually "Hilly."

Nixon: "Hilly"?

Chambers: Yes.

Nixon: Quite often?

Chambers: Yes.

Nixon: In your presence?

Chambers: Yes.

Nixon: Not "Alger"?

Chambers: Not "Alger."

Nixon: What nickname, if any, did Mr. Hiss use in addressing his wife?

Chambers: More often "Dilly" and sometimes "Pross." Her name was Priscilla. They were commonly referred to as "Hilly" and "Dilly."

Nixon: They were commonly referred to as "Hilly" and Dilly"?

Chambers: By other members of the group.

Nixon: You don't mean to indicate that was simply the nicknames used by the Communist group?

Chambers: This was a family matter.

Nixon: In other words, other friends and acquaintances of theirs would possibly have used these names? Did you ever spend any time in Hiss' home?

Chambers: Yes.

Nixon: Did you stay overnight?

Chambers: Yes; I stayed overnight for a number of days.

Nixon: You mean from time to time?

Chambers: From time to time.

Nixon: Did you ever stay longer than 1 day?

Chambers: I have stayed there as long as a week....

Nixon: Did the Hisses have any pets?

Chambers: They had, I believe, a cocker spaniel. I have a bad memory for dogs, but as nearly as I can remember it was a cocker spaniel.

Nixon: Do you remember the dog's name?

Chambers: No. I remember they used to take it up to some kennel. I think out Wisconsin Avenue.

Nixon: They took it to board it there?

Chambers: Yes. They made one or two vacation trips to the Eastern Shore of Maryland....

HUAC staff member Benjamin Mandel: Did Hiss have any hobbies?

Chambers: Yes; he did. They both had the same hobby—amateur ornithologists, bird observers. They used to get up early in the morning and go to Glen Echo, out the canal, to observe birds. I recall once they saw, to their great excitement, a prothonotary warbler.

John McDowell: A very rare specimen?

Chambers: I never saw one. I am also fond of birds....

Testimony of Alger Hiss, August 16, 1948

Nixon: As of course, Mr. Hiss, you are aware, the committee has a very difficult problem in regard to the testimony which has been submitted to the committee by Mr. Chambers and by yourself. The committee feels that it has the responsibility to resolve that problem as well as it can; and the purpose of this hearing and of the questions which the members of the committee will ask at this time is to assist the committee in resolving that particular problem....

As you have probably noted from press accounts of the hearings, Whittaker Chambers during the period that he alleges that he knew you was not known by the name of Whittaker Chambers. He has testified that he was known by the name of Carl. Do you recall having known an individual between the years 1934 and 1937 whose name was Carl?

Hiss: I do not recall anyone by the name of Carl that could remotely be connected with the kind of testimony Mr. Chambers has given....

Nixon: Your testimony, then, is that you have never known an individual solely by the name of Carl?

Hiss: That is correct, Mr. Nixon; that is my testimony....

Nixon: I am now showing you two pictures of Mr. Whittaker Chambers, also known as Carl, who testified that he knew you between the years 1934-37, and that he saw you in 1939. I ask you now, after looking at those pictures, if you can remember that person either as Whittaker Chambers or as Carl or as any other individual you have met.

Hiss: May I recall to the committee the testimony I gave in the public session when I was shown another photograph of Mr. Whittaker Chambers, and I had prior to taking the stand tried to get as many newspapers that had photographs of Mr. Chambers as I could.

I testified then that I could not swear that I had never seen the man whose picture was shown me. Actually the face has a certain familiarity. I think I also testified to that.

It is not according to the photograph a very distinctive or unusual face. I would like very much to see the individual face to face. I had hoped that would happen before. I still hope it will happen today.

I am not prepared to say that I have never seen the man whose pictures are now shown me. I said that when I was on the stand when a different picture was shown me. I cannot recall any person with distinctness and definiteness whose picture this is, but it is not completely unfamiliar.

Whether I am imagining that or not I don't know, but I certainly wouldn't want to testify without seeing the man, hearing him talk, getting some much more tangible basis for judging the person and the personality.

Nixon: Would your answer be any different if this individual were described to you as one who had stayed overnight in your house on several occasions?

Hiss: I think, Mr. Nixon, let me say this: In the course of my service in Government from 1933 to 1947 and the previous year 1929-30, and as a lawyer I have had a great many people who have visited in my house.

I have tried to recall in the last week or so anyone who would know my house whom I wouldn't know very well: There are many people that have come to my house on social occasions or on semibusiness occasions whom I probably wouldn't recall at all.

As far as staying overnight in my house is concerned—

Nixon: On several occasions.

Hiss: On several occasions.

Nixon: On several occasions.

Hiss: I can't believe, Mr. Nixon, that anyone could have stayed in my house when I was there—

Nixon: When you were there.

Hiss: —Overnight on several occasions without my being able to recall the individual; and if this is a picture of anyone, I would find it very difficult to believe that that individual could have stayed in my house when I was there on several occasions overnight and his face not be more familiar than it is….

Nixon: Mr. Hiss, let me explain this. Mr. Chambers, as indicated, did testify that he spent a week in your house. He also testified to other facts concerning his acquaintanceship with you—alleged facts, I should say—and I want to point out that the committee by getting answers to completely objective questions from you will be in a position to go certainly to third parties and to find out whether or not Mr. Chambers has committed perjury.

Now, on one point it is pretty clear that you have indicated that Mr. Chambers must have committed perjury because he said he spent a week in your house….

Hiss: May I say one thing for the record?

Nixon: Certainly.

Hiss: I have written a name on this pad in front of me of a person whom I knew in 1933 and 1934 who not only spent some time in my house but sublet my apartment. That man certainly spent more than a week, not while I was in the same apartment. I do not recognize the photographs as possibly being this man. If I hadn't seen the morning papers with an account of statements that he knew the inside of my house, I don't think I would even have thought of this name. I want to see Chambers face to face and see if he can be this individual. I do not want and I don't think I ought to be asked to testify now that man's name and everything I can remember about him....

Representative Felix Edward Hébert: As I say, I am not trying to be cagey or anything, but trying to put it on the line as certainly one member of this committee who has an open mind and up to this point don't know which one of the two is lying, but I will tell you right now and I will tell you exactly what I told Mr. Chambers so that will be a matter of record, too:

Either you or Mr. Chambers is lying.

Hiss: That is certainly true.

Hébert: And whichever one of you is lying is the greatest actor that America has ever produced. Now, I have not come to the conclusion yet which one of you is lying and I am trying to find the facts. Up to a few moments ago you have been very open, very cooperative. Now, you have hedged. You may be standing on what you consider your right and I am not objecting to that. I am not pressing you to identify a picture when you should be faced with the man. That is your right.... I can well appreciate the position you are in, but if I were in your position, I would do everything I humanly could to prove that Chambers is a liar instead of me....

Nixon: There are matters which I wish to go into now to which Mr. Chambers has given categorical answers. I am going to put the questions objectively, as you can see. I am not going to try to lead you one way or the other. It will be very helpful as the two records look together to see how accurate he is in this case.

I want to say first of all, so that it won't come up, that I realize that the matters which are covered are matters which third parties could corroborate, and that is the reason we ask these particular questions. Again for the purpose of just checking the veracity of Mr. Chambers and your testimony. It will help us to check it again.

What were the nicknames you and your wife had?

Hiss: My wife, I have always called her "Prossy."

Nixon: What does she call you?

Hiss: Well, at one time she called me quite frequently "Hill," H-i-l-l.

Nixon: What other name?

Hiss: "Hilly," with a "y."

Nixon: What other name did you call her? …

Hiss: She called me "Hill" or "Hilly." I called her "Pross" or "Prossy" almost exclusively. I don't think any other nickname.

Nixon: Did you ever call her "Dilly"?

Hiss: No; never.…

Nixon: Where did you spend your vacations during that period [of 1934 to 1937]?

Hiss: Normally, I think I didn't begin going to Peacham regularly until either 1937 or 1938; may have been 1937. My son went to a camp over on the Eastern Shore of Maryland. I am partly an Eastern Shore man myself. Part of my family came from there. When he was at camp we spent two summers, I think, during this period in Chestertown, Maryland.

Nixon: On the Eastern Shore?

Hiss: On the Eastern Shore of Maryland. He went to a camp of friends of ours who lived just outside of Chestertown. For two summers we took a small apartment.

Nixon: Did you have pets?

Hiss: We had a brown cocker spaniel we had before we came to Washington, was with us all during that period, and lived to be so old she died of old age.

Nixon: What did you do with the dog when you went on your vacations; do you recall?

Hiss: I think we took Tenny over on the Eastern Shore. I think we took her on the Eastern Shore when we went there. She did spend some time in the kennels when we were away.…

Nixon: What hobby, if any, do you have, Mr. Hiss?

Hiss: Tennis and amateur ornithology.

Nixon: Is your wife interested in ornithology?

Hiss: I also like to swim and also like to sail. My wife is interested in ornithology, as I am, through my interest. Maybe I am using too big a word to say an ornithologist because I am pretty amateur, but I have been interested in it since I was in Boston. I think anybody who knows me would know that.

John McDowell: Did you ever see a prothonotary warbler?

Hiss: I have right here on the Potomac. Do you know that place?

Chairman John Parnell Thomas: What is that?

Nixon: Have you ever seen one?

Hiss: Did you see it in the same place?

McDowell: I saw one in Arlington.

Hiss: They come back and nest in those swamps. Beautiful yellow head, a gorgeous bird.

Source: Chambers, Whittaker, and Alger Hiss, testimony of August 7, 1948, and August 16, 1948. House Committee on Un-American Activities, Hearings Regarding Communist Espionage in the United States Government, 80th Congress, 2nd Session. Washington, DC: Government Printing Office, 1948. Available online at http://www.law.umkc.edu/faculty/projects/ftrials/hiss/8-7testimony%5B1%5D.htm (Chambers testimony) and http://www.law.umkc.edu/faculty/projects/ftrials/hiss/8-16testimony.html (Hiss testimony).

The Speech That Launched McCarthy's Political Rise

On February 9, 1950, Senator Joseph McCarthy delivered a speech in Wheeling, West Virginia, that became one of the most famous political addresses in American history. In the speech, which was delivered to a local club of Republican women, McCarthy warned that Communists had infiltrated the U.S. State Department and many other important government agencies, and that they were actively plotting to destroy America. Most importantly, he declared that he knew the actual identities of many of these agents. McCarthy's declaration triggered a national uproar and instantly made him one of the most influential and controversial public figures in the United States.

Audience members in Wheeling reported that McCarthy claimed to know the names of 205 Reds in the U.S. government. But in the version of the speech that McCarthy inserted into the Congressional Record on February 20, 1950, his list contained fifty-seven names. The Congressional Record version of the speech is excerpted below.

Five years after a world war has been won, men's hearts should anticipate a long peace, and men's minds should be free from the heavy weight that comes with war. But this is not such a period—for this is not a period of peace. This is a time of the Cold War. This is a time when all the world is split into two vast, increasingly hostile armed camps—a time of a great armaments race. Today we can almost physically hear the mutterings and rumblings of an invigorated god of war. You can see it, feel it, and hear it all the way from the hills of Indochina, from the shores of Formosa right over into the very heart of Europe itself....

Today we are engaged in a final, all-out battle between communistic atheism and Christianity. The modern champions of communism have selected this as the time. And, ladies and gentlemen, the chips are down—they are truly down.

Lest there be any doubt that the time has been chosen, let us go directly to the leader of communism today—Joseph Stalin. Here is what he said—not back in 1928, not before the war, not during the war—but two years after the last war was ended: "To think that the communist revolution can be carried out peacefully, within the framework of a Christian democracy, means one has either gone out of one's mind and lost all normal understanding, or has grossly and openly repudiated the communist revolution."

And this is what was said by Lenin in 1919, which was also quoted with approval by Stalin in 1947: "We are living," said Lenin, "not merely in a state but in a system of states, and the existence of the Soviet Republic side by side with Christian states for a long time is unthinkable. One or the other must triumph in the end. And before that end supervenes, a series of frightful collisions between the Soviet Republic and the bourgeois states will be inevitable."

Ladies and gentlemen, can there be anyone here tonight who is so blind as to say that the war is not on? Can there be anyone who fails to realize that the communist world has said, "The time is now"—that this is the time for the showdown between the democratic Christian world and the communist atheistic world? Unless we face this fact, we shall pay the price that must be paid by those who wait too long.

Six years ago, at the time of the first conference to map out peace—Dumbarton Oaks—there was within the Soviet orbit 180 million people. Lined up on the anti-totalitarian side there were in the world at that time roughly 1.625 billion people. Today, only six years later, there are 800 million people under the absolute domination of Soviet Russia—an increase of over 400 percent. On our side, the figure has shrunk to around 500 million. In other words, in less than six years the odds have changed from 9 to 1 in our favor to 8 to 5 against us. This indicates the swiftness of the tempo of communist victories and American defeats in the Cold War. As one of our outstanding historical figures once said, "When a great democracy is destroyed, it will not be because of enemies from without but rather because of enemies from within." The truth of this statement is becoming terrifyingly clear as we see this country each day losing on every front.

At war's end we were physically the strongest nation on Earth and, at least potentially, the most powerful intellectually and morally. Ours could have been the honor of being a beacon in the desert of destruction, a shining, living proof that civilization was not yet ready to destroy itself. Unfortunately, we have failed miserably and tragically to arise to the opportunity.

The reason why we find ourselves in a position of impotency is not because our only powerful, potential enemy has sent men to invade our shores, but rather because of the traitorous actions of those who have been treated so well by this nation. It has not been the less fortunate or members of minority groups who have been selling this nation out, but rather those who have had all the benefits that the wealthiest nation on earth has had to offer—the finest homes, the finest college education, and the finest jobs in government we can give.

This is glaringly true in the State Department. There the bright young men who are born with silver spoons in their mouths are the ones who have been worst.

Now I know it is very easy for anyone to condemn a particular bureau or department in general terms. Therefore, I would like to cite one rather unusual case—the case of a man who has done much to shape our foreign policy.

When Chiang Kai-shek was fighting our war, the State Department had in China a young man named John S. Service. His task, obviously, was not to work for the communization of China. Strangely, however, he sent official reports back to the State Department urging that we torpedo our ally Chiang Kai-shek and stating, in effect, that communism was the best hope of China.

Later, this man—John Service—was picked up by the Federal Bureau of Investigation for turning over to the communists secret State Department information. Strangely, however, he was never prosecuted. However, Joseph Grew, the undersecretary of state, who insisted on his prosecution, was forced to resign. Two days after, Grew's successor, Dean Acheson, took over as undersecretary of state, this man—John Service—who had been picked up by the FBI and who had previously urged that communism was the best hope of China, was not only reinstated in the State Department but promoted; and finally, under Acheson, placed in charge of all placements and promotions. Today, ladies and gentlemen, this man Service is on his way to represent the State Department and Acheson in Calcutta—by far and away the most important listening post in the Far East.

Now, let's see what happens when individuals with communist connections are forced out of the State Department. Gustave Duran, who was labeled as, I quote, "a notorious international communist," was made assistant secretary of state in charge of Latin American affairs. He was taken into the State Department from his job as a lieutenant colonel in the Communist International Brigade. Finally, after intense congressional pressure and criticism, he resigned in 1946 from the State Department—and, ladies and gentlemen, where do you think he is now? He took over a high-salaried job as chief of the Cultural Activities Section in the office of the assistant secretary-general of the United Nations....

This, ladies and gentlemen, gives you somewhat of a picture of the type of individuals who have been helping to shape our foreign policy. In my opinion the State Department, which is one of the most important government departments, is thoroughly infested with communists.

I have in my hand 57 cases of individuals who would appear to be either card-carrying members or certainly loyal to the Communist Party, but who nevertheless are still helping to shape our foreign policy.

One thing to remember in discussing the Communists in our government is that we are not dealing with spies who get 30 pieces of silver to steal the blueprints of new weapons. We are dealing with a far more sinister type of activity because it permits the enemy to guide and shape our policy.

This brings us down to the case of one Alger Hiss, who is important not as an individual anymore but rather because he is so representative of a group in the State Department. It is unnecessary to go over the sordid events showing how he sold out the nation which had given him so much. Those are rather fresh in all of our minds. However, it should be remembered that the facts in regard to his connection with this international communist spy ring were made known to the then-Undersecretary of State Berle three days after Hitler and Stalin signed the Russo-German Alliance Pact. At that time one Whittaker Chambers—who was also part of the spy ring—apparently decided that with Russia on Hitler's side, he could no longer betray our nation to Russia. He gave Undersecretary of State Berle—and this is all a matter of record—practically all, if not more, of the facts upon which Hiss' conviction was based.

Undersecretary Berle promptly contacted Dean Acheson and received word in return that Acheson, and I quote, "could vouch for Hiss absolutely"—at which time the matter was dropped. And this, you understand, was at a time when Russia was an ally of Germany.

This condition existed while Russia and Germany were invading and dismembering Poland, and while the Communist groups here were screaming "warmonger" at the United States for their support of the Allied nations.

Again in 1943, the FBI had occasion to investigate the facts surrounding Hiss' contacts with the Russian spy ring. But even after that FBI report was submitted, nothing was done.

Then, late in 1948—on August 5—when the Un-American Activities Committee called Alger Hiss to give an accounting, President Truman at once issued a presidential directive ordering all government agencies to refuse to turn over any information whatsoever in regard to the communist activities of any government employee to a congressional committee.

Incidentally, even after Hiss was convicted, it is interesting to note that the president still labeled the exposé of Hiss as a "red herring."

If time permitted, it might be well to go into detail about the fact that Hiss was Roosevelt's chief adviser at Yalta when Roosevelt was admittedly in ill health and tired physically and mentally ... and when, according to the secretary of state, Hiss and Gromyko drafted the report on the conference.

According to the then-Secretary of State Stettinius, here are some of the things that Hiss helped to decide at Yalta: (1) the establishment of a European High Commission; (2) the treatment of Germany—this you will recall was the conference at which it was decided that we would occupy Berlin with Russia occupying an area completely encircling the city, which as you know, resulted in the Berlin airlift which cost 31 American lives; (3) the Polish question; (4) the relationship between UNRRA and the Soviet; (5) the rights of Americans on control commissions of Rumania, Bulgaria and Hungary; (6) Iran; (7) China—here's where we gave away Manchuria; (8) Turkish Straits question; (9) international trusteeships; (10) Korea.

Of the results of this conference, Arthur Bliss Lane of the State Department had this to say: "As I glanced over the document, I could not believe my eyes. To me, almost every line spoke of a surrender to Stalin."

As you hear this story of high treason, I know that you are saying to yourself, "Well, why doesn't the Congress do something about it?" Actually, ladies and gentlemen, one of the important reasons for the graft, the corruption, the dishonesty, the disloyalty, the treason in high government positions—one of the most important reasons why this continues—is a lack of moral uprising on the part of the 140 million American people. In the light of history, however, this is not hard to explain.

It is the result of an emotional hangover and a temporary moral lapse which follows every war. It is the apathy to evil which people who have been subjected to the tremendous evils of war feel. As the people of the world see mass murder, the destruction of defenseless and innocent people, and all of the crime and lack of morals which go with war, they become numb and apathetic. It has always been thus after war. However, the morals of our people have not been destroyed. They still exist. This cloak of numbness and apathy has only needed a spark to rekindle them. Happily, this spark has finally been supplied.

As you know, very recently the secretary of state proclaimed his loyalty to a man guilty of what has always been considered as the most abominable of all crimes—of being a traitor to the people who gave him a position of great trust. The secretary of state, in attempting to justify his continued devotion to the man who sold out the Christian world to the atheistic world, referred to Christ's Sermon on the Mount as a justification and reason therefore, and the reaction of the American people to this would have made the heart of Abraham Lincoln happy. When this pompous diplomat in striped pants, with a phony British accent, proclaimed to the American people that Christ on the Mount endorsed communism, high treason, and betrayal of a sacred trust, the blasphemy was so great that it awakened the dormant indignation of the American people.

He has lighted the spark which is resulting in a moral uprising and will end only when the whole sorry mess of twisted warped thinkers are swept from the national scene so that we may have a new birth of national honesty and decency in government.

Source: McCarthy, Joseph. Speech to Women's Republican Club, Wheeling, West Virginia, February 9, 1950. U.S. Senate, State Department Loyalty Investigation Committee on Foreign Relations, *Congressional Record*, 81st Congress, Second Session, February 20, 1950, p. 1956.

Margaret Chase Smith's Declaration of Conscience

When Senator Joseph McCarthy launched his crusade against alleged Communists in the U.S. State Department, Maine senator Margaret Chase Smith expressed support for his efforts. As time passed, however, she became increasingly disturbed by his tactics—and by the lack of evidence he presented to support his charges. By June 1950 Smith, who was the only female member of the Senate at the time, had become convinced that McCarthy posed a threat to the nation's well-being and unity. She and staff member William Lewis subsequently composed a "Declaration of Conscience" in which she denounced her fellow Republican for creating a national atmosphere of fear and distrust. Smith did not mention McCarthy by name in her address on the Senate floor, but the target of her message was clear to everyone present.

Six other moderate and liberal Republican senators formally endorsed Smith's warning (a seventh also signed on afterwards), but the rest of the Senate remained ominously silent. For his part, McCarthy ridiculed Smith and her cosigners as "Snow White and the Six Dwarfs," and he made no changes to his behavior. Today, her declaration (excerpted here) is regarded as a brave but ultimately failed bid to stop McCarthyism from spreading over the land.

Mr. President, I would like to speak briefly and simply about a serious national condition. It is a national feeling of fear and frustration that could result in national suicide and the end of everything that we Americans hold dear. It is a condition that comes from the lack of effective leadership in either the legislative branch or the executive branch of our Government....

I speak as a Republican. I speak as a woman. I speak as a United States Senator. I speak as an American.

The United States Senate has long enjoyed worldwide respect as the greatest deliberative body in the world. But recently that deliberative character has too often been debased to the level of a forum of hate and character assassination sheltered by the shield of congressional immunity.

It is ironical that we Senators can debate in the Senate directly or indirectly, by any form of words impute to any American, who is not a Senator, any conduct or motive unworthy or unbecoming an American—and without that non-Senator American having any legal redress against it—yet if we say the same thing in the Senate about our colleagues we can be stopped on the grounds of being out of order.

It is strange that we can verbally attack anyone else without restraint and with full protection and yet we hold ourselves above the same type of criticism here on the Senate floor. Surely the United States Senate is big enough to take self-criticism and self-appraisal. Surely we should be able to take the same kind of character attacks that we "dish out" to outsiders.

I think that it is high time for the United States Senate and its Members to do some soul searching—for us to weigh our consciences—on the manner in which we are performing our duty to the people of America; on the manner in which we are using or abusing our individual powers and privileges.

I think that it is high time that we remembered that we have sworn to uphold and defend the Constitution. I think that it is high time that we remembered that the Constitution, as amended, speaks not only of the freedom of speech, but also of trial by jury instead of trial by accusation.

Whether it be a criminal prosecution in court or a character prosecution in the Senate, there is little practical distinction when the life of a person has been ruined.

Those of us who shout the loudest about Americanism in making character assassinations are all too frequently those who, by our own words and acts, ignore some of the basic principles of Americanism—

The right to criticize;

The right to hold unpopular beliefs;

The right to protest;

The right of independent thought.

The exercise of these rights should not cost one single American citizen his reputation or his right to a livelihood nor should he be in danger of losing his reputation or livelihood merely because he happens to know someone who holds unpopular beliefs. Who of us doesn't? Otherwise none of us could call our souls our own. Otherwise thought control would have set in.

The American people are sick and tired of being afraid to speak their minds lest they be politically smeared as "Communists" or "Fascists" by their opponents. Freedom of speech is not what it used to be in America. It has been so abused by some that it is not exercised by others.

The American people are sick and tired of seeing innocent people smeared and guilty people whitewashed. But there have been enough proved cases, such as the Amerasia case, the Hiss case, the Coplon case, the Gold case, to cause Nation-wide distrust and strong suspicion that there may be something to the unproved, sensational accusations....

The record of the present Democratic administration has provided us with sufficient campaign issues without the necessity of resorting to political smears. America is rapidly losing its position as leader of the world simply because the Democratic administration has pitifully failed to provide effective leadership.

The Democratic administration has completely confused the American people by its daily contradictory grave warnings and optimistic assurances— that show the people that our Democratic administration has no idea of where it is going.

The Democratic administration has greatly lost the confidence of the American people by its complacency to the threat of communism here at home and the leak of vital secrets to Russia through key officials of the Democratic administration. There are enough proved cases to make this point without diluting our criticism with unproved charges.

Surely these are sufficient reasons to make it clear to the American people that it is time for a change and that a Republican victory is necessary to the security of this country. Surely it is clear that this nation will continue to suffer as long as it is governed by the present ineffective Democratic administration.

Yet to displace it with a Republican regime embracing a philosophy that lacks political integrity or intellectual honesty would prove equally disastrous to this Nation. The Nation sorely needs a Republican victory. But I don't want to see the Republican Party ride to political victory on the four horsemen of calumny [false and malicious statements]—fear, ignorance, bigotry and smear.

I doubt if the Republican Party could—simply because I don't believe the American people will uphold any political party that puts political exploitation above national interest. Surely we Republicans aren't that desperate for victory.

I don't want to see the Republican Party win that way. While it might be a fleeting victory for the Republican Party, it would be a more lasting defeat for the American people. Surely it would ultimately be suicide for the Republican Party and the two-party system that has protected our American liberties from the dictatorship of a one-party system.

As members of the minority party, we do not have the primary authority to formulate the policy of our Government. But we do have the responsibility of rendering constructive criticism, of clarifying issues, of allaying fears by acting as responsible citizens.

As a woman, I wonder how the mothers, wives, sisters, and daughters feel about the way in which members of their families have been politically mangled in Senate debate—and I use the word "debate" advisedly.

As a United States Senator, I am not proud of the way in which the Senate has been made a publicity platform for irresponsible sensationalism. I am not proud of the reckless abandon in which unproved charges have been hurled from this side of the aisle. I am not proud of the obviously staged, undignified countercharges that have been attempted in retaliation from the other side of the aisle.

I don't like the way the Senate has been made a rendezvous for vilification, for selfish political gain at the sacrifice of individual reputations and national unity. I am not proud of the way we smear outsiders from the floor of the Senate and hide behind the cloak of congressional immunity and still place ourselves beyond criticism on the floor of the Senate.

As an American, I am shocked at the way Republicans and Democrats alike are playing directly into the Communist design of "confuse, divide and conquer." As an American, I don't want a Democratic administration "whitewash" or "cover-up" any more than I want a Republican smear or witch hunt.

As an American, I condemn a Republican "Fascist" just as much as I condemn a Democrat "Communist." I condemn a Democrat "Fascist" just as much as I condemn a Republican "Communist." They are equally dangerous to you and me and to our country. As an American, I want to see our Nation recapture the strength and unity it once had when we fought the enemy instead of ourselves.

It is with these thoughts I have drafted what I call a Declaration of Conscience. I am gratified that the senator from New Hampshire [Charles W. Tobey], the senator from Vermont [George D. Aiken], the senator from Oregon [Wayne L. Morse], the senator from New York [Irving M. Ives], the senator from Minnesota [Edward J. Thye], and the senator from New Jersey [Robert C. Hendrickson] have concurred in that declaration and have authorized me to announce their concurrence.

Statement of Seven Republican Senators

re Republicans. But we are Americans first. It is as Americans
ss our concern with the growing confusion that threatens the
..ty and stability of our country. Democrats and Republicans alike have
contributed to that confusion.

2. The Democratic administration has initially created the confusion by
its lack of effective leadership, by its contradictory grave warnings and optimistic assurances, by its complacency to the threat of communism here at
home, by its oversensitiveness to rightful criticism, by its petty bitterness
against its critics.

3. Certain elements of the Republican Party have materially added to
this confusion in the hopes of riding the Republican Party to victory through
the selfish political exploitation of fear, bigotry, ignorance, and intolerance.
There are enough mistakes of the Democrats for Republicans to criticize con-
structively without resorting to political smears.

4. To this extent, Democrats and Republicans alike have unwittingly, but
undeniably, played directly into the Communist design of "confuse, divide
and conquer."

5. It is high time that we stopped thinking politically as Republicans and
Democrats about elections and started thinking patriotically as Americans
about national security based on individual freedom. It is high time that we
all stopped being tools and victims of totalitarian techniques—techniques
that, if continued here unchecked, will surely end what we have come to
cherish as the American way of life.

Source: Smith, Margaret Chase. "Declaration of Conscience" Statement of June 1, 1950,
Congressional Record, 82nd Congress, 1st Session. Washington, DC: Government
Printing Office, 1950, pp. 621-24. Available online at http://www.senate.gov/artand
history/history/resources/pdf/SmithDeclaration.pdf.

Julius and Ethel Rosenberg Receive Death Sentences for Treason

The trial of Julius and Ethel Rosenberg was one of the most significant events of the McCarthy era. When the couple was convicted of conspiracy to pass military secrets on to the Soviets in 1951, many Americans treated the verdict as solid confirmation that Reds had indeed infiltrated all levels of government and society. On April 5, 1951, Judge Irving Kaufman imposed the death sentence on both Rosenbergs for their crimes. His sentencing statement is excerpted below. The Rosenbergs appealed Kaufman's sentence, but their convictions and death sentences were upheld by the U.S. Circuit Court of Appeals on February 25, 1952. Julius and Ethel Rosenberg were executed on June 19, 1953.

Because of the seriousness of this case and the lack of precedence, I have refrained from asking the Government for a recommendation. The responsibility is so great that I believe that the Court alone should assume this responsibility....

The issue of punishment in this case is presented in a unique framework of history. It is so difficult to make people realize that this country is engaged in a life and death struggle with a completely different system. This struggle is not only manifested externally between these two forces but this case indicates quite clearly that it also involves the employment by the enemy of secret as well as overt outspoken forces among our own people. All of our democratic institutions are, therefore, directly involved in this great conflict. I believe that never at any time in our history were we ever confronted to the same degree that we are today with such a challenge to our very existence. The atom bomb was unknown when the espionage statute was drafted. I emphasize this because we must realize that we are dealing with a missile of destruction which can wipe out millions of Americans.

The competitive advantage held by the United States in super-weapons has put a premium on the services of a new school of spies—the homegrown variety that places allegiance to a foreign power before loyalty to the United States. The punishment to be meted out in this case must therefore serve the maximum interest for the preservation of our society against these traitors in our midst.

It is ironic that the very country which these defendants betrayed and sought to destroy placed every safeguard around them for obtaining a fair and impartial trial, a trial which consumed three weeks in this court. I recall the defendant Julius Rosenberg testifying that our American system of jurisprudence met with his approval and was preferred over Russian justice. Even the defendants realize—by this admission—that this type of trial would not have been afforded to them in Russia. Certainly, to a Russian national accused of a conspiracy to destroy Russia not one day would have been consumed in a trial. It is to America's credit that it took the pains and exerted the effort which it did in the trial of these defendants. Yet, they made a choice of devoting themselves to the Russian ideology of denial of God, denial of the sanctity of the individual, and aggression against free men everywhere instead of serving the cause of liberty and freedom.

I consider your crime worse than murder. Plain deliberate contemplated murder is dwarfed in magnitude by comparison with the crime you have committed. In committing the act of murder, the criminal kills only his victim. The immediate family is brought to grief and when justice is meted out the chapter is closed. But in your case, I believe your conduct in putting into the hands of the Russians the A-bomb years before our best scientists predicted Russia would perfect the bomb has already caused, in my opinion, the Communist aggression in Korea, with the resultant casualties exceeding 50,000 and who knows but that millions more of innocent people may pay the price of your treason. Indeed, by your betrayal you undoubtedly have altered the course of history to the disadvantage of our country. No one can say that we do not live in a constant state of tension. We have evidence of your treachery all around us every day—for the civilian defense activities throughout the nation are aimed at preparing us for an atom bomb attack.

Nor can it be said in mitigation of the offense that the power which set the conspiracy in motion and profited from it was not openly hostile to the United States at the time of the conspiracy. If this was your excuse the error of your ways in setting yourselves above our properly constituted authorities and the decision of those authorities not to share the information with Russia must now be obvious.

The evidence indicated quite clearly that Julius Rosenberg was the prime mover in this conspiracy. However, let no mistake be made about the role which his wife, Ethel Rosenberg, played in this conspiracy. Instead of deterring him from pursuing his ignoble cause, she encouraged and assisted the cause. She was a mature woman—almost three years older than her husband and almost seven years older than her younger brother. She was a full-fledged partner in this crime.

Indeed the defendants Julius and Ethel Rosenberg placed their devotion to their cause above their own personal safety and were conscious that they were sacrificing their own children, should their misdeeds be detected—all of which did not deter them from pursuing their course. Love for their cause dominated their lives—it was even greater than their love for their children.

What I am about to say is not easy for me. I have deliberated for hours, days and nights. I have carefully weighed the evidence. Every nerve, every fiber of my body has been taxed. I am just as human as are the people who have given me the power to impose sentence. I am convinced beyond any doubt of your guilt. I have searched the records—I have searched my conscience—to find some reason for mercy—for it is only human to be merciful and it is natural to try to spare lives. I am convinced, however, that I would violate the solemn and sacred trust that the people of this land have placed in my hands were I to show leniency to the defendants Rosenberg. It is not in my power, Julius and Ethel Rosenberg, to forgive you. Only the Lord can find mercy for what you have done.

The sentence of the Court upon Julius and Ethel Rosenberg is, for the crime for which you have been convicted, you are hereby sentenced to the punishment of death, and it is ordered upon some day within the week beginning with Monday, May 21st, you shall be executed according to law.

Source: Kaufman, Irving. "Sentencing of Julius and Ethel Rosenberg." Transcript of Record, *Julius Rosenberg and Ethel Rosenberg v. United States of America,* Supreme Court of the United States, October Term, 1951, pp. 1612-16. Reprinted in Schrecker, Ellen. *The Age of McCarthyism: A Brief History with Documents.* Boston: St. Martin's Press, 1994, pp. 144-46.

Ronald Reagan Assesses Hollywood's Progress against the Reds

The American film industry was profoundly shaken by congressional investigations of Communist influence during the 1940s and 1950s. Studios moved decisively to blacklist all performers, writers, and directors who bore the stain of Communism, and the film industry publicized these efforts far and wide. Actor (and future president) Ronald Reagan was a high-profile figure in the effort to bolster Hollywood's reputation with Congress and the moviegoing public. He was a "friendly witness" to the House Un-American Activities Committee (HUAC) and regularly spoke about his personal loathing for Communism. In July 1951 he also penned an article, reprinted here, in which he assured readers that Hollywood had successfully expunged all Communists from its ranks. But Reagan also urged the public not to be too hard on artists who had been "tricked" in the 1930s "into lending their names or giving money to organizations or causes that later proved to be influenced or dominated by communists."

C ommunism failed in Hollywood because the overwhelming majority of the members of the Screen Actors Guild, the Screen Extras Guild, the writers' and directors' guilds and the workers in the Hollywood studio craft unions are and always have been opposed to communism.

Day after day in this year's hearings by the House Committee on Un-American Activities, the same story has been unfolded—a story of communist frustration and failure in the party's bold plot to seize control of the talent guilds and craft unions, through which the subversive brethren hoped eventually to control contents of films and thus influence the minds of 80,000,000 movie goers.

The extent of Hollywood's victory over the Communist Party is all the more remarkable because Hollywood for many years was a prime target of the Red propagandists and conspirators in this country.

They were trying to carry out orders from Joseph Stalin, who had said: "The cinema is not only a vital agitprop [active propaganda] device for the education and political indoctrination of the workers, but is also a fluent channel through which to reach the minds and shape the desires of people everywhere. The Kinofikatsiya [turning propaganda into films] is inevitable. The task is to take this affair into your hands, and vigorously execute it in every field."

So the Red enemies of our country concentrated their big guns on Hollywood. And they failed completely. But not before they had succeeded in bringing about two years of disastrous strikes and bloody fighting in which

American workmen battled other American workmen at the studio gates. And, unfortunately, not before the communists had fooled some otherwise loyal Americans into believing that the Communist Party sought to make a better world. Those dupes know today that the real aim of the Communist Party is to try to prepare the way for Russian conquest of the world.

The Screen Actor Guild members are justifiably proud of the key role they played in bringing about the final defeat of the communist conspirators in Hollywood.

Actually, there were very few actors in Hollywood who became Party members. But there were quite a number who were tricked many years ago into lending their names or giving money to organizations or causes that later proved to be influenced or dominated by communists.

Today, even the fellow traveler has disappeared from the Hollywood scene.

But it was not so in 1945 and 1946 when the communist-backed Conference of Studio Unions battled with the anti-communist International Alliance of Theatrical Stage Employees, led by Richard Walsh and Roy Brewer.

To win, the Reds had to get the actors to join in the jurisdictional strike on the side of the strikers. If the actors didn't go to work, the studios would shut and the Reds would have won a great victory.

They tried every trick in the bag but the actors, led by the Board of Directors of Screen Actors Guild, out-thought them and out-fought them. We fought them on the record and off the record.

We fought them in meetings and behind the scenes.

Our Red foes even went so far as to threaten to throw acid in the faces of myself and some other stars, so that we "never would appear on the screen again." I packed a gun for some time and policemen lived at my home to guard my kids.

But that was more than five years ago and those days are gone forever, along with the deluded Red sympathizer and fellow traveler.

Never again can the communists hope to get anywhere in the movie capital. And it looks to me as if the die-hard Reds in this country are now concentrating their plotting in other industries such as defense plants. I hope that all such industries will take a leaf out of Hollywood's book and actively combat the communist conspirators wherever they may be found.

And any American who has been a member of the Communist Party at any time but who has now changed his mind and is loyal to our country should be willing to stand up and be counted; admit, "I was wrong," and give all the information he has to the government agencies who are combating the Red plotters.

We've gotten rid of the communist conspirators in Hollywood. Let's do it now in other industries!

Source: Reagan, Ronald. "Reds Beaten in Hollywood," *Citizen News*, July 30, 1951, pp. 18-20. Reprinted in Bentley, Eric. *Thirty Years of Treason: Excerpts from Hearings before the House Committee on Un-American Activities, 1938-1968.* New York: Viking, 1971, pp. 294-95.

Edward R. Murrow Takes on McCarthy

The March 9, 1954, broadcast of CBS's See It Now *news program was a significant event in Senator Joseph McCarthy's sliding political fortunes. The program was hosted by Edward R. Murrow, one of the nation's most respected journalists. Murrow and his staff dedicated the entire March 9 program to a scorching examination of McCarthy's investigative methods. Making extensive use of newsreels and audio tapes featuring McCarthy, Murrow asserted that the senator's anti-Communist tactics were inherently destructive and un-American. Three weeks later, McCarthy accepted an invitation to respond to the newsman's allegations on* See It Now, *but the senator's rebuttal failed to reverse the growing public disenchantment with him.*

The following is an excerpt from Murrow's historic broadcast (indented portions are quotes from audio tapes and newsreel footage used in the program).

Murrow: Good evening. Tonight "See It Now" devotes its entire half hour to a report on Senator Joseph R. McCarthy told mainly in his own words and pictures…. Our working thesis tonight is this question: If this fight against Communism is made a fight between America's two great political parties, the American people know that one of these parties will be destroyed, and the Republic cannot endure very long as a one party system.

We applaud that statement and we think Senator McCarthy ought to. He said it, seventeen months ago in Milwaukee.

> **McCarthy:** The American people realize that this cannot be made a fight between America's two great political parties. If this fight against Communism is made a fight between America's two great political parties, the American people know that one of those parties will be destroyed, and the Republic can't endure very long as a one party system.

Murrow: But on February 4th, 1954, Senator McCarthy spoke of one party's treason. This was at Charleston, West Virginia where there were no cameras running. It was recorded on tape.

> **McCarthy:** The issue between the Republicans and Democrats is clearly drawn. It has been deliberately drawn by those who

have been in charge of twenty years of treason. Now the hard
fact is ... those who wear the label "Democrat" wear it with
the stain of a historic betrayal....

Murrow: On one thing the Senator has been consistent. Often operating
as a one-man committee, he has traveled far, interviewed many, terrorized
some, accused civilian and military leaders of the past administration of a
great conspiracy to turn over the country to Communism, investigated and
substantially demoralized the present State Department, made varying
charges of espionage at Fort Monmouth. (The Army says it has been unable
to find anything relating to espionage there.) He has interrogated a varied
assortment of what he calls "Fifth Amendment Communists." Republican
Senator Flanders of Vermont said of McCarthy today: "He dons war paint; he
goes into his war dance; he emits his war whoops; he goes forth to battle and
proudly returns with the scalp of a pink army dentist." ...

[*The program then broadcasts excerpts from McCarthy's February 1954
questioning of decorated Army General Ralph Zwicker, which was criticized by
Republicans and Democrats alike.*]

Murrow: Then President Eisenhower issued a statement that his advisors thought censored the Senator, but the Senator saw it as another victory,
called the entire Zwicker case "a tempest in a teapot."

McCarthy: [If an] arrogant or witless man in a position of
power appears before our Committee and is found aiding the
Communist Party, he will be exposed. The fact that he might
be a General places him in no special class, as far as I am concerned. Apparently... the President and I now agree on the
necessity of getting rid of Communists. We apparently dis-
agree only on how we should handle those who protect Communists. When the shouting and the tumult dies, the American people and the President will realize that this unprecedented mud slinging against the Committee by the extreme
left wing elements of press and radio was caused solely
because another Fifth Amendment Communist was finally
dug out of the dark recesses and exposed to the public view.

Murrow (points to a chart): Senator McCarthy claims that only the left
wing press criticized him on the Zwicker case. Of the fifty large circulating news-

papers in the country, these are the left wing papers that criticized. These are the ones that supported him. The ratio is about three to one [against the Senator]. Now let us look at some of these "left wing" papers that criticized the Senator.

[*Murrow quotes from articles and headlines*]:

The Chicago Tribune: McCarthy will better serve his cause if he learns to distinguish the role of investigator from the role of avenging angel....

The New York Times: The unwarranted interference of a demagogue—a domestic Munich....

The Times Herald of Washington: Senator McCarthy's behavior towards Zwicker not justified....

The Herald Tribune of New York: McCarthyism involves assaults on basic Republican concepts....

The Milwaukee Journal: The line must be drawn and defended or McCarthy will become the government....

The Evening Star of Washington: It was a bad day for everyone who resents and detests the bully boy tactics which Senator McCarthy so often employs....

The New York World Telegram: Bamboozling, bludgeoning, distorting way....

St. Louis Post Dispatch: Unscrupulous, McCarthy bullying. What a tragic irony it is that the President's political advisors keep him from doing what every decent instinct must be commanding him to do....

Well, that's the ratio of a three-to-one, so-called "left-wing" press....

Murrow: And upon what meat doth Senator McCarthy feed? Two of the staples of his diet are the investigation, protected by immunity, and the half-truth. We herewith submit samples of both.

First, the half-truth. This was an attack on Adlai Stevenson at the end of the 1952 campaign. President Eisenhower, it must be said, had no prior knowledge of it.

TITLE: Chicago, Oct. 27, 1957

McCarthy: I perform this unpleasant task because the American people are entitled to have the coldly documented history of this man who says, "I want to be your President."

Strangely, Alger—I mean, Adlai [laughter]—But let's move on to another part of the jigsaw puzzle. Now, while you think— while you may think there can be no connection between the debonair Democrat candidate and a dilapidated Massachusetts barn, I want to show you a picture of this barn and explain the connection.

Here is the outside of the barn. Give me the pictures of the inside, if you will. Here is the outside of the barn up at Lee, Massachusetts. It looks as though it couldn't house a farmer's cow or goat. Here's the inside: a beautifully paneled conference room with maps of the Soviet Union. Well, in what way does Stevenson tie up with this?

My ... my investigators went out and took pictures of this barn after we had been tipped off of what was in it, tipped off that there was in this barn all the missing documents from the Communist front—IPR [Institute of Pacific Relations]—the IPR which has been named by the McCarran Committee ... named before the McCarran Committee as a cover shop for Communist espionage.

Now, let's take a look at a photostat of a document taken from the Massachusetts barn—one of those documents which was never supposed to see the light of day. Rather interesting it is. This is a document which shows that Alger Hiss and Frank Coe recommended Adlai Stevenson to the Mount Tremblant Conference which was called for the purpose of establishing foreign policy (post-war foreign policy) in Asia. Now, as you know, Alger Hiss is a convicted traitor. Frank Coe has been named under oath before congressional committees seven times as a member of the Communist Party. Why? Why do Hiss and Coe find that Adlai Stevenson is the man they want representing them at this conference? I don't know. Perhaps Adlai knows.

Murrow: But Senator McCarthy didn't permit his audience to hear the entire paragraph. This is the official record of the McCarran hearings. Anyone can buy it for two dollars. Here's a quote: "Another possibility for the Mount Tremblant conferences on Asia is someone from Knox's office or Stimson's office." (Frank Knox was our wartime Secretary of the Navy; Henry Stimson our Secretary of the Army, both distinguished Republicans.) And it goes on: "Coe and Hiss mentioned Adlai Stevenson, one of Knox's special assistants, and Harvey Bundy—former Assistant Secretary of State under Hoover, and now assistant to Stimson—because of their jobs."

We read from this documented record, not in defense of Mr. Stevenson, but in defense of truth. Specifically, Mr. Stevenson's identification with that red barn was no more, no less than that of Knox, Stimson or Bundy. It should be stated that Mr. Stevenson was once a member of the Institute of Pacific Relations. But so were such other loyal Americans as Senator Ferguson, John Foster Dulles, Paul Hoffman, Harry Luce and Herbert Hoover. Their association carries with it no guilt, and that barn has nothing to do with any of them.

Now, a sample of an investigation. The witness was Reed Harris, for many years a civil servant in the State Department, directing the Information Service. Harris was accused of helping the Communistic cause by curtailing some broadcasts to Israel. Senator McCarthy summoned him and questioned him about a book he had written in 1932.

> **McCarthy:** May we come to order. Mr. Reed Harris? Your name is Reed Harris?
>
> **Harris:** That's correct.
>
> **McCarthy:** You wrote a book in '32, is that correct?
>
> **Harris:** Yes, I wrote a book. And as I testified in executive session …
>
> **McCarthy:** At the time you wrote the book—pardon me; go ahead. I'm sorry. Proceed.
>
> **Harris:** At the time I wrote the book, the atmosphere in the universities of the United States was greatly affected by the Great Depression then in existence. The attitudes of students, the attitudes of the general public, were considerably different than they are at this moment, and for one thing there certainly was generally no awareness, to the degree that there is today, of the way the Communist Party works.
>
> **McCarthy:** You attended Columbia University in the early thirties. Is that right?

Harris: I did, Mr. Chairman.

McCarthy: Will you speak a little louder, sir?

Harris: I did, Mr. Chairman.

McCarthy: And were you expelled from Columbia?

Harris: I was suspended from classes on April 1st, 1932. I was later reinstated, and I resigned from the University.

McCarthy: And you resigned from the University. Did the Civil—Civil Liberties Union provide you with an attorney at that time?

Harris: I had many offers of attorneys, and one of those was from the American Civil Liberties Union, yes.

McCarthy: The question is did the Civil Liberties Union supply you with an attorney?

Harris: They did supply an attorney.

McCarthy: The answer is yes?

Harris: The answer is yes.

McCarthy: You know the Civil Liberties Union has been listed as "a front for, and doing the work of," the Communist Party?

Harris: Mr. Chairman this was 1932.

McCarthy: Yeah, I know it was 1932. Do you know that they since have been listed as a front for, and doing the work of the Communist Party?

Harris: I do not know that they have been listed so, sir.

McCarthy: You don't know they have been listed?

Harris: I have heard that mentioned or read that mentioned.

McCarthy: Now, you wrote a book in 1932. I'm going to ask you again: at the time you wrote this book, did you feel that professors should be given the right to teach sophomores that marriage—and I quote—"should be cast out of our civilization as antiquated and stupid religious phenomena?" Was that your feeling at that time?

Harris: My feeling was that professors should have the right to express their considered opinions on any subject, whatever they were, sir.

McCarthy: All right, I'm going to ask you this question again.

Harris: That includes that quotation. They should have the right to teach anything that came into their minds as being the proper thing to teach.

McCarthy: I'm going to make you answer this.

Harris: All right, I'll answer yes, but you put an implication on it, and you feature this particular point of the book, which, of course, is quite out of context, does not give a proper impression of the book as a whole. The American public doesn't get an honest impression of even that book, bad as it is, from what you are quoting from it.

McCarthy: Well, then, let's continue to read your own writing, and …

Harris: Twenty-one years ago, again.

McCarthy: Yes, but we shall try and bring you down to date, if we can.

Harris: Mr. Chairman, two weeks ago, Senator Taft took the position that I took twenty-one years ago, that Communists and Socialists should be allowed to teach in the schools. It so happens that nowadays I don't agree with Senator Taft, as far as Communist teaching in the schools is concerned, because I think Communists are, in effect, a plainclothes auxiliary of the Red Army, the Soviet Red Army. And I don't want to see them in any of our schools, teaching.

McCarthy: I don't recall Senator Taft ever having any of the background that you've got, sir.

Harris: I resent the tone of this inquiry very much, Mr. Chairman. I resent it, not only because it is my neck, my public neck, that you are, I think, very skillfully trying to wring, but I say it because there are thousands of able and loyal employees in the federal government of the United States who have been properly cleared according to the laws and the security practices of their agencies, as I was—unless the new regime says no; I was before.

Senator John McClellan: Do you think this book that you wrote then did considerable harm, its publication might have had adverse influence on the public by an expression of views contained in it?

Harris: The sale of that book was so abysmally small, it was so unsuccessful that a question of its influence…. Really, you can go back to the publisher. You'll see it was one of the most unsuccessful books he ever put out. He's still sorry about it, just as I am.

Senator John McClellan: Well, I think that's a compliment to American intelligence…. (Laughter). I will say that for him.

Murrow: Senator McCarthy succeeded in proving that Reed Harris had once written a bad book, which the American people had proved twenty-two years ago by not buying it, which is what they eventually do with all bad ideas. As for Reed Harris, his resignation was accepted a month later with a letter of commendation. McCarthy claimed it as a victory.

The Reed Harris hearing demonstrates one of the Senator's techniques. Twice he said the American Civil Liberties Union was listed as a subversive front. The Attorney General's list does not and has never listed the ACLU as subversive, nor does the FBI or any other federal government agency. And the American Civil Liberties Union holds in its files letters of commendation from President Truman, President Eisenhower, and General MacArthur….

Earlier, the Senator asked, "Upon what meat does this, our Caesar, feed?" Had he looked three lines earlier in Shakespeare's Caesar, he would have found this line, which is not altogether inappropriate: "The fault, dear Brutus, is not in our stars, but in ourselves."

No one familiar with the history of this country can deny that congressional committees are useful. It is necessary to investigate before legislating, but the line between investigating and persecuting is a very fine one and the junior Senator from Wisconsin has stepped over it repeatedly. His primary achievement has been in confusing the public mind, as between the internal and the external threats of Communism. We must not confuse dissent with disloyalty. We must remember always that accusation is not proof and that conviction depends upon evidence and due process of law. We will not walk in fear, one of another. We will not be driven by fear into an age of unreason, if we dig deep in our history and our doctrine, and remember that we are not descended from fearful men—not from men who feared to write, to speak, to associate and to defend causes that were, for the moment, unpopular.

This is no time for men who oppose Senator McCarthy's methods to keep silent, or for those who approve. We can deny our heritage and our history, but we cannot escape responsibility for the result. There is no way for a citizen of a republic to abdicate his responsibilities. As a nation we have come into our full inheritance at a tender age. We proclaim ourselves, as indeed we are, the defenders of freedom, wherever it continues to exist in the world, but we cannot defend freedom abroad by deserting it at home.

The actions of the junior Senator from Wisconsin have caused alarm and dismay amongst our allies abroad, and given considerable comfort to our enemies. And whose fault is that? Not really his. He didn't create this situation of fear; he merely exploited it—and rather successfully. Cassius was right. "The fault, dear Brutus, is not in our stars, but in ourselves."

Good night, and good luck.

Source: Murrow, Edward R., and CBS News. *See It Now.* Transcribed 7/20/06 by G. Handman from DVD, *The McCarthy Years* (Edward R. Murrow Collection). Available online at University of California (Berkeley) Media Resources Center, Moffitt Library, http://www.lib.berkeley.edu/MRC/murrowmccarthy.html.

The Army-McCarthy Hearings Bring McCarthy Down

On March 16, 1954, the Senate Committee on Government Operations convened its Permanent Subcommittee on Investigations to review the charges of misconduct that the U.S. Army and Senator Joseph McCarthy had leveled against each other. These so-called "Army-McCarthy hearings" convened on April 22, 1954, and ran until June 17, 1954. The nationally televised hearings attracted huge numbers of Americans who were spellbound by the legal jousting between McCarthy and his chief aide, Roy Cohn, on one side, and special counsel for the Army Joseph N. Welch and counsel for the Army John G. Adams on the other.

McCarthy's public image gradually eroded during the hearings, but one clash in particular was responsible for crushing the senator's reputation beyond repair. That exchange (excerpted below) took place on June 9, when Welch was cross-examining Cohn in a mocking tone about McCarthy and Cohn's assertions that the Army Signal Corps facility at Monmouth, New Jersey, was rife with Communists. McCarthy suddenly interrupted the questioning to accuse Welch of harboring a Communist sympathizer at his law firm. Welch's devastating response to this accusation sent McCarthy on his final downward spiral into political oblivion.

Welch: If you could be God and do anything you wished, you would cure [the problem of Communist infiltrators in the Army] by sundown, wouldn't you?

Cohn: Yes, sir.

Welch: And you were that alarmed about Monmouth?

Cohn: It doesn't go that way.

Welch: I am just asking how it does go. When you find there are Communists and possible spies in a place like Monmouth, you must be alarmed, aren't you?

Cohn: Now you have asked me how it goes, and I am going to tell you.

Welch: No; I didn't ask you how it goes. I said aren't you alarmed when you find it is there?

Cohn: Whenever I hear that people have been failing to act on FBI information about Communists, I do think it is alarming, I would like the Communists out, and I would like to be able to advise this committee of why people who have the responsibility for getting them out haven't carried out their responsibility.

Welch: Yes, but what you want first of all, Mr. Cohn, and let's be fair with each other, what you want first of all, if it is within your power, is to get them out, isn't it?

Cohn: I don't know if I draw a distinction as to what ought to come first, Mr. Welch.

Welch: It certainly ranks terrifically high, doesn't it?

Cohn: It was a situation that I thought should be developed, and we did develop it.

Welch: When did you first meet [Army] Secretary Stevens?

Cohn: I first met Secretary Stevens September 7 I believe it was....

Welch: And on September 7, when you met him, you had in your bosom this alarming situation about Monmouth, is that right?

Cohn: Yes; I knew about Monmouth, then. Yes, sir.

Welch: And you didn't tug at his lapel and say, "Mr. Secretary, I know something about Monmouth that won't let me sleep nights"? You didn't do it, did you?

Cohn: I don't—as I testified, Mr. Welch, I don't know whether I talked to Mr. Stevens about it then or not. I know that on the 16th I did. Whether I talked to him on the 7th or not, is something I don't know.

Welch: Don't you know that if you had really told him what your fears were, and substantiated them to any extent, he could have jumped in the next day with suspensions?

Cohn: No, sir.

Welch: Did you then have any reason to doubt his fidelity?

Cohn: No, sir.

Welch: Or his honor?

Cohn: No.

Welch: Or his patriotism?

Cohn: No.

Welch: And yet, Mr. Cohn, you didn't tell him what you knew?

Cohn: I don't know whether I did or not. I told him some of the things I knew, sir. I don't think I told him everything I knew on the first occasion.

After the first 2 or 3 occasions, I think he had a pretty good idea of what we were working on.

Welch: Mr. Cohn, tell me once more: Every time you learn of a Communist or a spy anywhere, is it your policy to get them out as fast as possible?

Cohn: Surely, we want them out as fast as possible, sir.

Welch: And whenever you learn of one from now on, Mr. Cohn, I beg of you, will you tell somebody about them quick?

Cohn: Mr. Welch, with great respect, I work for the committee here. They know how we go about handling situations of Communist infiltration and failure to act on FBI information about Communist infiltration. If they are displeased with the speed with which I and the group of men who work with me proceed, if they are displeased with the order in which we move, I am sure they will give me appropriate instructions along those lines, and I will follow any which they give me.

Welch: May I add my small voice, sir, and say whenever you know about a subversive or a Communist spy, please hurry. Will you remember those words?

McCarthy: Mr. Chairman.

Cohn: Mr. Welch, I can assure you, sir, as far as I am concerned, and certainly as far as the chairman of this committee and the members, and the members of the staff, are concerned, we are a small group, but we proceed as expeditiously as is humanly possible to get out Communists and traitors and to bring to light the mechanism by which they have been permitted to remain where they were for so long a period of time.

McCarthy: Mr. Chairman, in view of that question—

[Committee Chairman Karl] Mundt: Have you a point of order?

McCarthy: Not exactly, Mr. Chairman, but in view of Mr. Welch's request that the information be given once we know of anyone who might be performing any work for the Communist Party, I think we should tell him that he has in his law firm a young man named Fisher whom he recommended, incidentally, to do work on this committee, who has been for a number of years a member of an organization which was named, oh, years and years ago, as the legal bulwark of the Communist Party, an organization which always swings to the defense of anyone who dares to expose Communists. I certainly assume that Mr. Welch did not know of this young man at the time he recommended him as the assistant counsel for this committee, but he has such terror and such a great desire to know where anyone is located who may be serving the Communist cause, Mr. Welch, that I thought we should just call to your attention the fact that your Mr. Fisher, who is still in your law firm today, whom you asked to have down here looking over the secret and classified material, is a member of an organization, not named by me but named by various committees, named by the Attorney General, as I recall, and I think I quote this verbatim, as "the legal bulwark of the Communist Party." He belonged to that for a sizable number of years, according to his own admission, and he belonged to it long after it had been exposed as the legal arm of the Communist Party.

Knowing that, Mr. Welch, I just felt that I had a duty to respond to your urgent request that before sundown, when we know of anyone serving the Communist cause, we let the agency know. We are now letting you know that your man did belong to this organization for, either 3 or 4 years, belonged to it long after he was out of law school.

I don't think you can find anyplace, anywhere, an organization which has done more to defend Communists—I am again quoting the report—to defend Communists, to defend espionage agents, and to aid the Communist cause, than the man whom you originally wanted down here at your right hand instead of Mr. St. Clair.

I have hesitated bringing that up, but I have been rather bored with your phony requests to Mr. Cohn here that he personally get every Communist out of government before sundown. Therefore, we will give you information about the young man in your own organization.

I am not asking you at this time to explain why you tried to foist him on this committee. Whether you knew he was a member of that Communist organization or not, I don't know. I assume you did not, Mr. Welch, because I get the impression that, while you are quite an actor, you play for a laugh, I don't think you have any conception of the danger of the Communist Party. I don't think you yourself would ever knowingly aid the Communist cause. I think you are unknowingly aiding it when you try to burlesque this hearing in which we are attempting to bring out the facts, however.

Welch: Mr. Chairman.

Mundt: Mr. Welch, the Chair should say he has no recognition or no memory of Mr. Welch's recommending either Mr. Fisher or anybody else as counsel for this committee.

I will recognize Mr. Welch.

McCarthy: Mr. Chairman, I will give you the news story on that.

Welch: Mr. Chairman, under these circumstances I must have something approaching a personal privilege.

Mundt: You may have it, sir. It will not be taken out of your time.

Welch: Senator McCarthy, I did not know—Senator, sometimes you say "May I have your attention?"

McCarthy: I am listening to you. I can listen with one ear.

Welch: This time I want you to listen with both.

McCarthy: Yes.

Welch: Senator McCarthy, I think until this moment—

McCarthy: Jim, will you get the news story to the effect that this man belonged to this Communist-front organization? Will you get the citations showing that this was the legal arm of the Communist Party, and the length of time that he belonged, and the fact that he was recommended by Mr. Welch? I think that should be in the record.

Welch: You won't need anything in the record when I have finished telling you this.

Until this moment, Senator, I think I never really gauged your cruelty or your recklessness. Fred Fisher is a young man who went to the Harvard Law School and came into my firm and is starting what looks to be a brilliant career with us.

When I decided to work for this committee I asked Jim St. Clair, who sits on my right, to be my first assistant. I said to Jim, "Pick somebody in the firm who works under you that you would like." He chose Fred Fisher and they came down on an afternoon plane. That night, when he had taken a little stab at trying to see what the case was about, Fred Fisher and Jim St. Clair and I went to dinner together. I then said to these two young men, "Boys, I don't know anything about you except I have always liked you, but if there is anything funny in the life of either one of you that would hurt anybody in this case you speak up quick."

Fred Fisher said, "Mr. Welch, when I was in law school and for a period of months after, I belonged to the Lawyers Guild," as you have suggested,

Senator. He went on to say, "I am secretary of the Young Republicans League in Newton with the son of Massachusetts' Governor, and I have the respect and admiration of the 25 lawyers or so in Hale & Dorr."

I said, "Fred, I just don't think I am going to ask you to work on the case. If I do, one of these days that will come out and go over national television and it will just hurt like the dickens."

So, Senator, I asked him to go back to Boston.

Little did I dream you could be so reckless and cruel as to do an injury to that lad. It is true he is still with Hale & Dorr. It is true that he will continue to be with Hale & Dorr. It is, I regret to say, equally true that I fear he shall always bear a scar needlessly inflicted by you. If it were in my power to forgive you for your reckless cruelty, I will do so. I like to think I am a gentleman, but your forgiveness will have to come from someone other than me.

McCarthy: Mr. Chairman.

Mundt: Senator McCarthy?

McCarthy: May I say that Mr. Welch talks about this being cruel and reckless. He was just baiting; he has been baiting Mr. Cohn here for hours, requesting that Mr. Cohn, before sundown, get out of any department of Government anyone who is serving the Communist cause.

I just give this man's record, and I want to say, Mr. Welch, that it has been labeled long before he became a member, as early as 1944—

Welch: Senator, may we not drop this? We know he belonged to the Lawyers Guild, and Mr. Cohn nods his head at me. I did you, I think, no personal injury, Mr. Cohn.

Cohn: No, sir.

Welch: I meant to do you no personal injury, and if I did, beg your pardon.

Let us not assassinate this lad further, Senator. You have done enough. Have you no sense of decency sir, at long last? Have you left no sense of decency?

McCarthy: I know this hurts you, Mr. Welch. But I may say, Mr. Chairman, on a point of personal privilege, and I would like to finish it—

Welch: Senator, I think it hurts you, too, sir.

McCarthy: I would like to finish this.

Mr. Welch has been filibustering this hearing, he has been talking day after day about how he wants to get anyone tainted with communism out before sundown. I know Mr. Cohn would rather not have me go into this. I intend to, however, Mr. Welch talks about any sense of decency. If I say anything which is not the truth, then I would like to know about it....

I have heard you and every one else talk so much about laying the truth upon the table that when I hear—and it is completely phony, Mr. Welch, I have listened to you for a long time—when you say "Now, before sundown, you must get these people out of Government," I want to have it very clear, very clear that you were not so serious about that when you tried to recommend this man for this committee.

And may I say, Mr. Welch, in fairness to you, I have reason to believe that you did not know about his Communist-front record at the time you recommended him. I don't think you would have recommended him to the committee, if you knew that.

I think it is entirely possible you learned that after you recommended him.

Mundt: The Chair would like to say again that he does not believe that Mr. Welch recommended Mr. Fisher as counsel for this committee, because he has through his office all the recommendations that were made. He does not recall any that came from Mr. Welch, and that would include Mr. Fisher.

McCarthy: Let me ask Mr. Welch. You brought him down, did you not, to act as your assistant?

Welch: Mr. McCarthy, I will not discuss this with you further. You have sat within 6 feet of me, and could have asked me about Fred Fisher. You have brought it out. If there is a God in heaven, it will do neither you nor your cause any good. I will not discuss it further. I will not ask Mr. Cohn any more questions. You, Mr. Chairman, may, if you will, call the next witness.

Source: U.S. Senate, Committee on Government Operations, *Special Senate Investigation on Charges and Countercharges Involving Secretary of the Army Robert T. Stevens, John G. Adams, H. Struve Hensel and Senator Joe McCarthy, Roy M. Cohn, and Francis P. Carr*, 83rd Congress, 2nd Session, part 59. Washington: U.S. Government Printing Office, 1954, pp 2425-30. Available online at http://www.archive.org/stream/specialsenate inv59unit#page/n33/mode/2up.

The Senate Condemns McCarthy

Throughout the fall of 1954 the U.S. Senate debated a resolution that formally condemned Senator Joseph McCarthy for "dishonorable" conduct. A final resolution of censure reached the floor of the Senate for a vote on December 2. The language of the resolution mentioned only a few recent examples of actions by McCarthy that were "contrary to senatorial traditions," but the bill was universally regarded as a referendum on McCarthy's actions over the previous three and a half years. The resolution, reprinted below, passed by a 67-22 vote.

*R*esolved, that the senator from Wisconsin, Mr. McCarthy, failed to cooperate with the Subcommittee on Privileges and Elections of the Senate Committee on Rules and Administration in clearing up matters referred to that subcommittee which concerned his conduct as a senator and affected the honor of the Senate and, instead, repeatedly abused the subcommittee and its members who were trying to carry out assigned duties, thereby obstructing the constitutional processes of the Senate; and that this conduct of the senator from Wisconsin, Mr. McCarthy, is contrary to senatorial traditions and is hereby condemned.

Section 2. The senator from Wisconsin, Mr. McCarthy, in writing to the chairman of the Select Committee to Study Censure Charges (Mr. Watkins) after the Select Committee had issued its report and before the report was presented to the Senate charging three members of the Select Committee with "deliberate deception" and "fraud" for failure to disqualify themselves; in stating to the press on Nov. 4, 1954, that the special Senate session that was to begin Nov. 8, 1954, was a "lynch party"; in repeatedly describing this special Senate session as a "lynch bee" in a nationwide television and radio show on Nov. 7, 1954; in stating to the public press on Nov. 13, 1954, that the chairman of the Select Committee (Mr. Watkins) was guilty of "the most unusual, most cowardly thing I've heard of," and stating further: "I expected he would be afraid to answer the questions, but didn't think he'd be stupid enough to make a public statement"; and in characterizing the said committee as the "unwitting handmaiden," "involuntary agent," and "attorneys in fact" of the Communist Party, and in charging that the said committee in writing its report "imitated Communist methods—that it distorted, misrepresented, and omitted in its effort to manufacture a plausible rationalization" in support of its recommendations to the Senate, which characterizations and charges were contained in a statement released to the press and inserted in the *Congressional Record* of Nov. 10, 1954, acted contrary to senatorial ethics and tended to bring the Senate into dishonor and disrepute, to obstruct the constitutional processes of the Senate, and to impair its dignity; and such conduct is hereby condemned.

Source: Senate Resolution 301, 83rd Congress, 2nd Session, December 2, 1954. Available online at http://www.ourdocuments.gov/doc.php?flash=true&doc=86&page= transcript.

Playwright Arthur Miller Recalls the McCarthy Era

In 1952 playwright Arthur Miller wrote The Crucible, *one of the most famous plays in the history of the American stage. In the play, Miller used the Salem witchcraft trials of the 1690s as an allegory for the hunt for Communists that was being waged across America by Senator Joseph McCarthy and his allies.* The Crucible *opened on Broadway in 1953, at the height of McCarthyism. It initially received a mixed reception from American critics and audiences, but it is now recognized as a classic work of the American theatre. In this excerpt from a 1967 essay, Miller gives his impressions of the McCarthy era. He also speculates about America's continued vulnerability to the fear-stoking manipulations of men and women like McCarthy.*

I keep no file of reviews, but if memory serves, *The Crucible* was generally dismissed as a cold, anti-McCarthy tract, more an outburst than a play. A relatively small band of rooters kept it on the Broadway stage for six months or so.

It is certain that a reading now of those reviews would leave unexplained, to say the least, why the play has continued to be produced here and around the world these fifteen years, or why it should have run through several seasons in France and remains in many permanent repertories, including Olivier's National Theatre in Britain. There have been years when it was more often performed than *Death of a Salesman*. Something living must thrive in the play which, I was told on its opening, was a dead husk.

Perhaps its victory over adversities has made me prouder of it than of anything else I have written, and perhaps it is permissible to say why I think it has refused to be dismissed.

The prime point at issue in 1953 when it opened was whether the analogy was a sound one between the Massachusetts witch hunt and the then-current hysteria about Communists boring from within the government, labor, education, entertainment and the intellectual community. After all, there never were any witches while there certainly were Communists, so that *The Crucible* appeared to some as a misreading of the problem at best—a "naïvete," or at worst a specious and even sinister attempt to whitewash the guilt of the Communists with the noble heroism of those in 1692 who had

---

rather be hanged than confess to nonexistent crimes. Indeed, the critic Eric Bentley wrote that one never knew what a Miller play was about.

I believe that life does provide some sound analogies now and again, but I don't think they are any good on the stage. Before a play can be "about" something else, it has to be about itself. If *The Crucible* is still alive, it can hardly be due to any analogy with McCarthyism. It is received in the same way in countries that have never known such a wave of terror as those that have. The bulk of the audiences, for example, in the British National Theatre, are too young to have known McCarthyism, and England is not a hysterical country. Nor, quite rightly, is it for them a play about a "problem" to be "solved."

The truth is that as caught up as I was in opposition to McCarthyism, the playwriting part of me was drawn to what I felt was a tragic process underlying the political manifestation. It is a process as much a part of humanity as walls and food and death, and no play will make it go away. When irrational terror takes to itself the fiat of moral goodness, somebody has to die. I thought then that in terms of this process the witch hunts had something to say to the anti-Communist hysteria. No man lives who has not got a panic button and when it is pressed by the clean white hand of moral duty, a certain murderous train is set in motion. Socially speaking this is what the play is and was "about," and it is this which I believe makes it survive long after the political circumstances of its birth have evaporated in the public mind.

Is it a political play? It is, I think, but in a particular sense. It is very often done in Latin America just before a dictatorship is about to take over—as a warning—and just after one has been overthrown, as a reminder. It was one of the first foreign works to be done after Stalin's death, and I will wager that it will be done soon after Franco goes to his reward. As I say, it is very popular in England, where hysteria is not one of the national vices. I think it is a political play but not in terms of Left and Right. Its underlying reference is to political paranoia, whichever side makes use of that source of power.

But paranoid politics is not easy to discuss for the reason that *our* fears are always based on something quite palpable and real, while *theirs* are illusory. I realize now that it was probably impossible to have expected an audience and critics in 1953 to feel the heat of a play which so much as implied that a state of deep fear was not entirely new in the world, let alone that the evil plotters might just be worth some dispassionate examination. On top of this, to have treated this fear as a tragic thing rather than a necessary and realistic and highly moral sort of patriotism, was more than could be borne by liberals and conservatives alike.

We customarily think of paranoia as a craziness, a diseased delusionary state in which fears are obviously out of proportion to any conceivable stimulus. But if this were all, we should never be endangered by it. Paranoia has a power and it rises not basically from ravings about plots and hidden conspiracies, but from the grain of recognizable fact around which the fantasies are woven.

The paranoid feels endangered by some person or group mysteriously controlling his actions despite his will. His violence is therefore always defensive, trained against oppressors who mean to kill him before he can kill them. His job is therefore to unmask and disarm, to find the seemingly innocent traces of the pervading malevolence, and he comes to recognize hostility even in the way a person folds his hands or turns his head. His only hope is power, power to neutralize the dangers around him. Naturally, since those dangers can be anywhere, his power must also be total in order to work.

And of course it is true that to one degree or another we are, in fact, hostile to each other, and when we are accused of holding that hostility, we do indeed hate the accusation and the accuser. So that the paranoid creates the reality which proves him right. And this is why the paranoid, who in normal times might merely end in an institution, can rise to the leadership of a society which is really insecure and at a loss as to the causes of its spiritual debility. Nothing is as frightening as to not know why one is frightened. Given the "cause" we can act, and thus keep ourselves from flying apart altogether.

Paranoid politics is seductive, too, because all politics requires that we symbolize people, until individuals cease to exist and there are only compliant supporters or the opposition. The paranoid discovers the murderous potential in the opposition, which it therefore must destroy. When, during World War II, for example, we ripped 100,000 Japanese-Americans out of their California farms and shops and confined them to Midwestern camps, we were indulging the paranoid side of our realistic fears of Japan. But was it really probably that *all* these men, women and children were secret agents? The grain of truth was that some, or perhaps one of them, was. Their non-"whiteness" enhanced our irrationality; we never rounded up German-Americans even though crowds of them, unlike the Japanese, had been marching around with Nazi flags in Jersey right up to the day we declared war.

A few years after its original production, *The Crucible* opened again in New York, Off-Broadway, and the script was now judged by many of the same critics as an impassioned play rather than a cold tract, and it ran two years. It is true that the original production was formalized and rather ballet-like, but not by that much. It was simply that in 1958 nobody was afraid any more. Nor do I imagine that I can convince many people that this is basically what was changed and for good reason. Great fear, like great pain, is not easily recalled, it is self-healing, and the more of it we have felt the less of it we can really get ourselves to remember. And this forgetfulness is part of the tragedy.

But no amount of paranoids walking around has very great political significance unless a partner appears who, naturally, is Interest. Hitler without the support of German big business would have merged with the legions of the mentally lost. Stalin in his last years slept in a different bed every night, employed food-tasters, and ordered the executions of people whose names he merely heard in conversation, but if the Revolution had created a healthy, ongoing society, it could not have tolerated such a chief. Had the witch-crying girls started their shenanigans in a stable community certain of itself and its future, they would have been soaked in cold water and put to bed.

But land titles were in dispute in Salem due to edicts from Boston and London; the repressions of the Puritan code no longer seemed holy to people born after the early deprivations of the militant pioneers. A host of socially disruptive pressures were upon Salem which seemed to threaten a disorder beyond the power of the mind to analyze. The girls lifted up a cause for it all out of the morass. Americans in the late forties and fifties felt paralyzed before a power of darkness expanding its reign; we had "lost" China (which we had never "had") and Eastern Europe. Enormous Communist parties existed in France and Italy. McCarthy solved the problem of our helplessness with a stroke—we were infiltrated by the enemy. Twenty years of conservative frustration with contemporary America was unleashed until, like the girls, McCarthy was in a position of such incredible authority that the greatest people in the land shuddered at the thought that their names might fall from his sniggering lips.

The fantasy of the fifties has rich documentation, but the Rosenberg case, because it ended in death, provides one insight which may throw some light on paranoid fear. In the final speech of the presiding judge is the statement that the defendants committed one of the gravest crimes in all history in giving the atom-bomb secret to Russia. Yet, no expert competent to make such a judgment had been called, and even more instructive—the defense attorney was so eager to prove *his* adherence to the reigning fear that he moved to impound the diagram of the bomb lens allegedly transmitted by the Rosenbergs, so that nobody in the future could steal it again—or, by the way, examine its validity. Recently, however, it was examined by a group of physicists who had actually worked on the lens, and their verdict was that it was scientifically a farce. I am reasonably sure that the passion of the judge's speech was real, and certainly he was not crazy. He was, however, afraid.

Can it all happen again? I believe it can. Will it?

The opposite of paranoid politics is Law and good faith. An example, the best I know, is the American Constitution, and the Bill of Rights, which de-symbolize the individual and consider him as the sum of his acts rather than his hidden thoughts and propensities for plotting evil.

And there are signs that somehow, someway, people in responsible positions have learned at least part of the lesson. Despite our being in a war [the Vietnam War], despite the immense opposition to it, the draft-card burning and demonstrations, the President [Lyndon B. Johnson] and the leadership of the country as a whole have not rallied the unwashed to go hunting for people whose bad thoughts are cheating us of victory.

But what will happen if the American becomes more desperately frustrated, if this war goes on for years, if a sense of national powerlessness prepared the ground for cries of "Betrayal!"—the old paranoid cry to which the highly moral mad respond by seeing where others are blind.

Laws, as we know, are made of bendable stuff; panic systematized around a grain of fact waits forever in the human brain. The tragic reply, John Proctor's, is unfortunately, no defense against this kind of social dissolution, but spoken in good time it is perhaps our only safety: "A fire, a fire is burning. I hear the boot of Lucifer, I see his filthy face. And it is my face, and yours, Danforth. For them that quail to bring men out of ignorance as I have quailed, and as you do now when you know in all your black hearts that this be fraud—God damns our kind especially...." A foisted analogy? Only if we are certain the slide into darkness is far, far behind us. As things stand, Proctor's passion has its own life intact and will until Power is guaranteed against the temptations of the irrational. The surgeons say they work to make their job unnecessary. *The Crucible* was written in that spirit—that the coiled thing in the public heart might die of light. A reasonable thought, but an unreasonable hope which against all reason never disappears.

Source: Miller, Arthur. "It Could Happen Here—and Did." *New York Times*, April 30, 1967, Sec. 2, p. 17. Reprinted in *The Theater Essays of Arthur Miller.* New York: Viking Press/Penguin Books, 1978, pp. 294-300.

A Conservative Writer Defends the Legitimacy of Questions about the "al-Qaeda Seven"

In March 2010 a conservative political organization called Keep America Safe, led by activists Liz Cheney and Debra Burlingame and pundit William Kristol, produced a video questioning the loyalty and patriotism of officials in President Barack Obama's Justice Department. Specifically, the group demanded to know the identities of seven lawyers in the Justice Department who had previously "represented or advocated for terrorist detainees" associated with al-Qaeda, the terrorist outfit that committed the 9/11 attacks on America.

One day after the video was released, the identities of the seven officials in question were revealed by Fox News, then confirmed by the Justice Department. The release of this information, however, did nothing to dampen a storm of protests from Democrats and liberal groups that the Keep America Safe video was nothing more than a despicable twenty-first-century version of McCarthyism. Keep America Safe also was rebuked by a group of conservative lawyers and legal scholars, including several former high-ranking officials of the George W. Bush administration. This group released a letter that described attacks on the Justice Department lawyers as "shameful" and reminded citizens that "the American tradition of zealous representation of unpopular clients is at least as old as John Adams' representation of the British soldiers charged in the [1770] Boston Massacre."

This criticism from fellow conservatives stung the Keep America Safe organization, but it refused to disavow the video. "The American people have a right to know who in the Department of Justice is setting policy regarding detention of terrorists and related national security issues," said executive director Aaron Harison.[1] Many other conservative writers and politicians rushed to the group's defense as well. One such person was Marc A. Thiessen, a political commentator who served as a speechwriter to both Secretary of State Donald Rumsfeld and President George W. Bush. He strongly defended the video in a column, reprinted below, that appeared in the March 8, 2010, edition of the Washington Post. *One day later, liberal* Washington Post *columnist Eugene Robinson harshly criticized the organization and video* (see p. 195).

Would most Americans want to know if the Justice Department had hired a bunch of mob lawyers and put them in charge of mob cases? Or a group of drug cartel lawyers and put them in charge of drug cases? Would they want their elected representatives to find out who these lawyers were, which mob bosses and drug lords they had worked for,

---

and what roles they were now playing at the Justice Department? Of course they would—and rightly so.

Yet Attorney General Eric Holder hired former al-Qaeda lawyers to serve in the Justice Department and resisted providing Congress this basic information. In November, Republicans on the Senate Judiciary Committee sent Holder a letter requesting that he identify officials who represented terrorists or worked for organizations advocating on their behalf, the cases and projects they worked on before coming to the Justice Department, the cases and projects they've worked on since joining the administration, and a list of officials who have recused themselves because of prior work on behalf of terrorist detainees.

Holder stonewalled for nearly three months. Finally, two weeks ago, he admitted that nine political appointees in the Justice Department had represented or advocated for terrorist detainees, but he failed to identify seven whose names were not publicly known or to directly answer other questions the senators posed. So Keep America Safe, a group headed by Liz Cheney, posted a Web ad demanding that Holder identify the "al-Qaeda seven," and a subsequent Fox News investigation unearthed the names. Only under this public pressure did the Justice Department confirm their identities—but Holder still refuses to disclose their roles in detention policy.

Americans have a right to this information. One lawyer in the National Security Division of Holder's Justice Department, Jennifer Daskal, has written that any terrorist not charged with a crime "should be released from Guantanamo's system of indefinite detention" even though "at least some of these men may ... join the battlefield to fight U.S. soldiers and our allies another day." Should a lawyer who advocates setting terrorists free, knowing they may go on to kill Americans, have any role in setting U.S. detention policy? My hunch is that most Americans would say no.

Do other lawyers in question hold similarly radical and dangerous views? Without the information Holder is withholding, we cannot know if such lawyers are affecting detainee policy.

Yet for raising questions, Cheney and the Republican senators have been vilified. Former Clinton Justice Department official Walter Dellinger decried the "shameful" personal attacks on "these fine lawyers," while numerous commentators leveled charges of "McCarthyism."

Where was the moral outrage when fine lawyers like John Yoo, Jay Bybee, David Addington, Jim Haynes, Steve Bradbury and others came under vicious personal attack? Their critics did not demand simple transparency; they demanded heads. They called these individuals "war criminals" and sought to have them fired, disbarred, impeached, and even jailed. Where were the defenders of the "al-Qaeda seven" when a Spanish judge tried to indict the "Bush six"? Philippe Sands, author of the "Torture Team," crowed: "This is the end of these people's professional reputations!" I don't recall anyone accusing him of "shameful" personal attacks.

The standard today seems to be that you can say or do anything when it comes to the Bush lawyers who defended America against the terrorists. But if you publish an Internet ad or ask legitimate questions about Obama administration lawyers who defended America's terrorist enemies, you are engaged in a McCarthyite witch hunt.

Some defenders say al-Qaeda lawyers are simply following a great American tradition, in which everyone gets a lawyer and their day in court. Not so, says Andy McCarthy, the former assistant U.S. attorney who put Omar Abdel Rahman, the "blind sheik," behind bars for the 1993 World Trade Center bombing. "We need to be clear about what the American tradition is," McCarthy told me. "The Sixth Amendment guarantees the accused — that means somebody who has been indicted or otherwise charged with a crime — a right to counsel. But that right only exists if you are accused, which means you are someone who the government has brought into the civilian criminal justice system." The habeas lawyers were not doing their constitutional duty to defend unpopular criminal defendants. They were using the federal courts as a tool to undermine our military's ability to keep dangerous enemy combatants off the battlefield in a time of war.

If lawyers who once sought to free captured terrorists are now setting U.S. policy when it comes to the release of Guantanamo detainees, moving terrorists to the United States, trying senior al-Qaeda leaders in civilian courts, and whether to give captured terrorists Miranda rights, then, as Sen. Chuck Grassley (R-Iowa) put it, the public has "a right to know who advises the attorney general and the president on these critical matters." Only when this information is public can members of Congress judge whether these individuals have properly recused themselves or whether they should be involved in detainee matters at all. The charge of McCarthyism is intended to intimidate those raising legitimate questions into silence. But asking such questions is not McCarthyism. It's oversight.

Source: Thiessen, Marc A. "The 'al-Qaeda Seven' and Selective McCarthyism," *Washington Post*, March 8, 2010.

Notes

[1] Quoted in Schwartz, John. "Attacks on Detainee Lawyers Split Conservatives," *New York Times,* March 9, 2010.

A Liberal Columnist Condemns the "al-Qaeda Seven" Video as Modern-Day McCarthyism

In March 2010 a conservative political organization called Keep America Safe released a video that expressed doubts about the loyalty and patriotism of officials in President Barack Obama's Justice Department. The video claimed that seven unknown lawyers in the Justice Department had previously "represented or advocated for terrorist detainees" associated with al-Qaeda, the terrorist outfit that committed the 9/11 attacks on America. One day after the video was released, Fox News revealed the identities of the seven officials targeted in the video.

The affair unleashed a barrage of angry protests from Democrats and liberal groups that the Keep America Safe video was a shameless example of twenty-first-century McCarthyism. The following essay by Washington Post *columnist Eugene Robinson provides a fairly representative sample of reaction to the video and the Keep America Safe organization from the political left. This column appeared on March 9, 2010—one day after former presidential speechwriter Marc A. Thiessen defended the video on the editorial pages of the same paper (see p. 192).*

T he word "McCarthyism" is overused, but in this case it's mild. Liz Cheney, the former vice president's ambitious daughter, has in her hand a list of Justice Department lawyers whose "values" she has the gall to question. She ought to spend the time examining her own principles, if she can find them.

A group that Liz Cheney co-chairs, called Keep America Safe, has spent the past two weeks scurrilously attacking the Justice Department officials because they "represented or advocated for terrorist detainees" before joining the administration. In other words, they did what lawyers are supposed to do in this country: ensure that even the most unpopular defendants have adequate legal representation and that the government obeys the law.

Liz Cheney is not ignorant, and neither are the other co-chairs of her group, advocate Debra Burlingame and pundit William Kristol, who writes a monthly column for The Post. Presumably they know that "the American tradition of zealous representation of unpopular clients is at least as old as John

Adams' representation of the British soldiers charged in the Boston Massacre"—in other words, older than the nation itself.

That quote is from a letter by a group of conservative lawyers—including several former high-ranking officials of the Bush-Cheney administration, legal scholars who have supported draconian detention and interrogation policies, and even Kenneth W. Starr—that blasts the "shameful series of attacks" in which Liz Cheney has been the principal mouthpiece. Among the signers are Larry Thompson, who was deputy attorney general under John Ashcroft; Peter Keisler, who was acting attorney general for a time during George W. Bush's second term; and Bradford Berenson, who was an associate White House counsel during Bush's first term.

"To suggest that the Justice Department should not employ talented lawyers who have advocated on behalf of detainees maligns the patriotism of people who have taken honorable positions on contested questions," the letter states.

But maligning is apparently the whole point of the exercise. The smear campaign by Cheney, et al., has nothing to do with keeping America safe. It can only be an attempt to inflict political damage on the Obama administration by portraying the Justice Department as somehow "soft" on terrorism. Even by Washington's low standards, this is unbelievably dishonest and dishonorable.

"Whose values do they share?" a video on the group's Web site ominously asks. The answer is obvious: the values enshrined in the U.S. Constitution.

The most prominent of the nine Justice officials, Principal Deputy Solicitor General Neal Katyal, represented Osama bin Laden's driver, Salim Hamdan, in a case that went to the Supreme Court. In a 5-to-3 decision, the court sided with Hamdan and ruled that the Bush administration's military tribunals were unconstitutional. Are Liz Cheney and her pals angry that Katyal was right? Or do they also question the "values" and patriotism of the five justices who voted with the majority?

The letter from the conservative lawyers points out that "in terrorism detentions and trials alike, defense lawyers are playing, and will continue to play, a key role." It notes that whether terrorism suspects are tried in civilian or military courts, they will have access to counsel—and that Guantanamo inmates, even if they do not face formal charges, have a right to habeas corpus review of their detention. It is the federal courts—not defense lawyers—

that have made all of this crystal clear. If Cheney and her group object, they should prepare a blanket denunciation of the federal judiciary. Or maybe what they really don't like is that pesky old Constitution, with all its checks, balances and guarantees of due process. How inconvenient to live in a country that respects the rule of law.

But there I go again, taking the whole thing seriously. This is really part of a death-by-a-thousand-cuts strategy to wound President Obama politically. The charge of softness on terrorism—or terrorist suspects—is absurd; Obama has brought far more resources and focus to the war against al-Qaeda in Afghanistan than the Bush-Cheney administration cared to summon. Since Obama's opponents can't attack him on substance, they resort to atmospherics. They distort. They insinuate. They sully. They blow smoke.

This time, obviously, they went too far. But the next Big Lie is probably already in the works. Scorched-earth groups like Keep America Safe may just be pretending not to understand our most firmly established and cherished legal principles, but there is one thing they genuinely don't grasp: the concept of shame.

Source: Robinson, Eugene. "'Al-Qaeda 7' Smear Campaign Is an Assault on American Values," *Washington Post*, March 9, 2010.

IMPORTANT PEOPLE, PLACES, AND TERMS

Alien Registration Act *see* **Smith Act**

Bentley, Elizabeth (1908-1963)
American spy for the Soviet Union who in 1945 renounced her Communist ties and cooperated with federal investigators.

Bolshevik
A member of the Russian Social Democratic Workers' Party that seized power in Russia in 1917; also often used to describe any Communist.

Chambers, Whittaker (1901-1965)
American writer and ex-Communist who accused State Department official Alger Hiss of being a Soviet agent.

Cohn, Roy (1927-1986)
Lawyer and chief aide to Joseph McCarthy.

Cold War
A period of intense political and military rivalry between the United States and Soviet Union that began in the aftermath of World War II and lasted until the breakup of the Soviet Union in 1991.

Comintern
An association of Communist parties around the world that was directed by Soviet leaders in Moscow.

Communism
A political system in which the state controls all economic activity, distributes resources evenly among the populace, and exerts significant control over citizens' rights and freedoms.

Dies, Martin (1900-1972)
First chairman of the House Un-American Activities Committee.

Eisenhower, Dwight D. (1890-1969)
Thirty-fourth president of the United States, from 1953 to 1961.

Fellow Traveler
An individual who was not an actual member of the American Communist Party, but who was supportive of its policies or worked on its behalf.

Fifth Amendment
Constitutional amendment in the Bill of Rights that states that no citizen may be forced to testify against himself or herself in a court of law.

Fifth column
A secret undercover group or organization that works within a country to undermine its economic or political foundations for the benefit of an external enemy.

Hatch Act
A law passed in 1939 that made loyalty to the United States a condition of federal employment and paved the way for secret "loyalty" screenings and investigations.

Hiss, Alger (1904-1996)
Former State Department official who was accused of being a Soviet spy, and who ultimately was convicted of related charges.

Hollywood Ten
Group of ten film industry writers and directors who were blacklisted for refusing to cooperate with the House Un-American Activities Committee.

Hoover, J. Edgar (1895-1972)
Director of the Federal Bureau of Investigation (FBI) from 1924 to 1972.

House Un-American Activities Committee (HUAC)
A committee within the U.S. House of Representatives, established in 1938, to investigate Communist propaganda and activities. Originally better known as the Dies Committee, after its first chairman, Martin Dies.

HUAC *see* House Un-American Activities Committee

Internal Security Act *see* McCarran Act

Left
Individuals or organizations that hold liberal political beliefs; also left-wing.

McCarran Act
Legislation passed in 1950 that required all Communist organizations to register with the U.S. government and established legality of heightened investigations and prosecutions of "radicals" and "subversives."

McCarthy, Joseph (1908-1957)
U.S. senator from Wisconsin who led the anti-Communist "witch hunts" of the early 1950s in America.

McCarthyism
Irresponsibly accusing individuals or groups of disloyalty to country without solid evidence.

Miller, Arthur (1915-2005)
Playwright whose works included *The Crucible,* which was highly critical of McCarthyism.

Murrow, Edward R. (1908-1965)
News journalist who broadcast an editorial strongly condemning Senator Joseph McCarthy in 1954.

New Deal
Term used to refer to the wide range of programs and policies introduced by the Franklin D. Roosevelt administration to promote economic recovery and social reform during the Great Depression.

Palmer, A. Mitchell (1872-1936)
U.S. attorney general from 1919 to 1921 who supervised the anti-radical Palmer Raids.

Palmer Raids
Series of raids conducted in 1919 and 1920 by the Justice Department against "radicals."

Pearson, Drew (1897-1969)

American journalist and syndicated columnist who became one of Senator Joseph McCarthy's most prominent critics.

Radical

Revolutionary or extreme political and social views or a person who holds such views.

Red-baiting

Accusing or prosecuting an individual for being a Communist or holding Communist sympathies. Often associated with accusations that have little or no evidence to back them up.

Reds

Communists or Socialists.

Red Scare

Periods during which fear and anxiety about Communism are high in American society.

Right

Individuals or organizations that hold conservative political beliefs; also right-wing.

Rosenberg, Julius (1918-1953) and Ethel (1915-1953)

Americans who were executed in 1953 for passing military secrets to the Soviets.

Schine, G. David (1927-1996)

Army private and former senatorial aide who became a central figure in the Army-McCarthy hearings of 1954.

Smith, Margaret Chase (1897-1995)

Republican senator from Maine (1949-1973) who authored an anti-McCarthy "Declaration of Conscience."

Smith Act

A 1940 statute, also known as the Alien Registration Act, that made it illegal to call or advocate for overthrow of the U.S. government.

Socialism

A political and economic system based on government or community-wide ownership of industry and resources rather than private ownership.

Thomas, J. Parnell (1895-1970)
Republican congressman from New Jersey who chaired the House Un-American Activities Committee from mid-1947 through 1949.

Truman, Harry S. (1884-1972)
Thirty-third president of the United States, from 1945 to 1953.

Truman Doctrine
Foreign policy stance announced by President Harry S. Truman in 1947 that emphasized containment of Communism.

Venona Project
Top secret code-breaking project, which deciphered the texts of intercepted telegraphic correspondence between operatives in the United States and their Moscow superiors.

Welch, Joseph N. (1890-1960)
Chief counsel for the U.S. Army during the Army-McCarthy hearings.

CHRONOLOGY

1917

Bolsheviks take control of Russia in the Russian Revolution.

The United States passes the Espionage Act of 1917.

1919

The Communist International or Comintern is formed in Moscow to coordinate Communist activities in other countries; later that year the American Communist Party is founded.

In November the U.S. Justice Department launches the first of the Palmer Raids against alleged Communists and other political radicals.

1922

The Soviet Union (USSR) is established.

1924

J. Edgar Hoover becomes the director of the Federal Bureau of Investigation (FBI).

1933

President Franklin D. Roosevelt launches his New Deal programs of social welfare and reform.

1935

The Comintern ends its isolation from other political groups and cultivates an anti-Fascist image.

1938

The House Un-American Activities Committee (HUAC) is established. In its earliest years of operation it is widely known as the Dies Committee.

1939

The United States implements the Hatch Act, which makes loyalty to the United States a condition of federal employment.

1940

The U.S. government begins "loyalty" screenings of federal employees.

Congress passes the Smith Act, also known as the Alien Registration Act, to stamp out Communist and Nazi activity in America.

1941

The United States enters World War II on the side of the Soviet Union and other Allied nations.

1945

President Roosevelt dies and is succeeded by Harry S. Truman.

The Allied powers win World War II and establish post-war boundaries and other treaty agreements in Europe; subsequent Soviet expansionism triggers the beginning of the Cold War between the Soviet Union and the United States.

1946

Republicans gain control of both houses of Congress.

1947

Truman announces the creation of the Truman Doctrine to halt Communist expansion.

Truman signs Executive Order 9835, which establishes a loyalty program for all federal employees.

The Hollywood Ten hearings commence before the House Un-American Activities Committee in October.

Hollywood studios issue the Waldorf Statement on December 3.

1948

The House Un-American Activities Committee begins hearings into the Alger Hiss–Whittaker Chambers dispute.

Truman wins re-election.

1949

In August the Soviet Union successfully detonates an atomic bomb, an event that greatly heightens American fears of Communism.

1950

Alger Hiss is convicted of perjury in January on charges related to accusations that he was a Soviet agent during his years in the State Department.

On February 9 Wisconsin senator Joseph McCarthy issues his famous speech about Communists in the State Department at Wheeling, West Virginia.

Washington Post editorial cartoonist Herbert Block, better known as Herblock, coins the term "McCarthyism" in a March 29 cartoon.

Senator Margaret Chase Smith delivers her Declaration of Conscience speech against McCarthy on June 1.

McCarthy attacks World War II hero George Marshall on June 14 in a widely criticized speech.

The Korean War begins on June 25.

The Tydings Committee issues a withering report on McCarthy, but the Senate takes no action.

The McCarran Act is passed by Congress over the veto of President Truman.

1951

Julius and Ethel Rosenberg are sentenced to death after being convicted of being Soviet spies.

1952

Supreme Court justice William O. Douglas decries the "Black Silence of Fear" created by McCarthyism in an editorial in the *New York Times*.

November election results send Republican Dwight Eisenhower to the White House, increase Republican majorities in Congress, and boost McCarthy's political influence.

McCarthy is given chairmanship of the Permanent Subcommittee on Investigations (PSI) of the Government Operations Committee; this subcommittee becomes McCarthy's primary vehicle for his anti-Communist investigations.

1953

Arthur Miller's anti-McCarthyism play *The Crucible* opens on Broadway.

Roy Cohn joins the Permanent Subcommittee on Investigations and becomes McCarthy's top aide.

Julius and Ethel Rosenberg are executed on June 19.

The Korean War ends on July 27.

McCarthy announces in the fall that he intends to investigate Communist infiltration of the U.S. Army.

1954

During the March 9 broadcast of the CBS news program *See It Now*, journalist Edward R. Murrow delivers a searing indictment of McCarthy's investigative methods and his overall impact on American society.

The nationally televised Army-McCarthy hearings begin on April 22.

A June 9 clash at the Army-McCarthy hearings between McCarthy and Army chief counsel Joseph N. Welch culminates with Welch's famous "have you no decency?" speech.

The Army-McCarthy hearings end on June 17 with Senator McCarthy's reputation in tatters.

The U.S. Senate votes on December 2 to condemn McCarthy.

1956

FBI director J. Edgar Hoover launches the secret COINTELPRO program to conduct surveillance (often illegally) against domestic political organizations.

1957

McCarthy dies on May 2 of acute hepatitis of the liver.

1971

The FBI's COINTELPRO program is terminated after a wave of adverse publicity.

1975

The U.S. House of Representatives abolishes the House Un-American Activities Committee.

2001

The USA Patriot Act is signed into law by President George W. Bush on October 26.

SOURCES FOR FURTHER STUDY

Doherty, Tim. *Cold War, Cool Medium: Television, McCarthyism, and American Culture.* New York: Columbia University Press, 2003. The author, a noted film historian, provides a fascinating examination of the many ways in which America's young television industry knuckled under to McCarthyism—before finally striking back in 1954 and contributing to Senator Joseph McCarthy's political ruin.

Fried, Albert. *Communism in America: A History in Documents.* New York: Columbia University Press, 1997. This work collects a wide range of primary sources that trace the history of organized Communist activity in the United States. Selections are organized by historical period and supplemented with informative headnotes.

Haynes, John Earl, and Harvey Klehr. "The Alger Hiss–Whittaker Chambers Case." In *Early Cold War Spies: The Espionage Trials That Shaped American Politics.* New York: Cambridge University Press, 2006. This chapter, written by two eminent Cold War historians, provides a clear overview of perhaps the most famous spy case in U.S. history.

McCarthyism/The "Red Scare." Dwight D. Eisenhower Presidential Library. Available online at http://www.eisenhower.archives.gov/research/digital_documents/mccarthy/mccarthy documents.html. This Web resource compiled by the staff of the Eisenhower Presidential Library contains background information on Eisenhower's tense relationship with Senator Joseph McCarthy, as well as many presidential documents relating to McCarthyism and the 1950s-era Red Scare.

Wicker, Tom. *Shooting Star: The Brief Arc of Joe McCarthy.* New York: Harcourt, 2006. A slim, fast-paced, and highly readable biography of the Wisconsin senator by a former political reporter and columnist for the *New York Times.*

BIBLIOGRAPHY

Books

Ackerman, Kenneth D. *Young J. Edgar: Hoover, the Red Scare, and the Assault on Civil Liberties.* Cambridge, MA: Da Capo Press, 2008.

Caute, David. *The Great Fear: The Anti-Communist Purge under Truman and Eisenhower.* New York: Simon and Schuster, 1978.

Daniels, Roger. *Guarding the Golden Door: American Immigration Policy and Immigrants since 1882.* New York: Hill and Wang, 2004.

Evans, M. Stanton. *Blacklisted by History: The Untold Story of Senator Joe McCarthy and His Fight against America's Enemies.* New York: Crown Forum, 2007.

Fariello, Griffin. *Red Scare: Memories of the American Inquisition.* New York: Norton, 1995.

Fried, Albert. *McCarthyism: The Great American Red Scare: A Documentary History.* New York: Oxford University Press, 1996.

Fried, Richard M. *Nightmare in Red: The McCarthy Era in Perspective.* New York: Oxford University Press, 1991.

Gaddis, John Lewis. *We Now Know: Rethinking Cold War History.* New York: Oxford University Press, 1997.

Goldman, Eric F. *The Crucial Decade—and After: America, 1945-1960.* New York: Vintage Books, 1960.

Griffith, Robert. *The Politics of Fear: Joseph R. McCarthy and the Senate.* Lexington: University Press of Kentucky, 1970; 2nd ed., Amherst: University of Massachusetts Press, 1987.

Haynes, John Earl. *Red Scare or Red Menace? American Communism and Anticommunism in the Cold War Era.* Chicago: Ivan R. Dee, 1996.

Haynes, John Earl, Harvey Klehr, and Alexander Vassiliev. *Spies: The Rise and Fall of the KGB in America.* New Haven, CT: Yale University Press, 2009.

Heale, M. J. *American Anticommunism: Combating the Enemy Within, 1830-1970.* Baltimore: Johns Hopkins University Press, 1990.

Herman, Arthur. *Joseph McCarthy: Reexamining the Life and Legacy of America's Most Hated Senator.* New York: Free Press, 1999.

Higham, John. *Strangers in the Land: Patterns of American Nativism, 1860-1925.* Rev. ed. New Brunswick, NJ: Rutgers University Press, 2002.

Jacoby, Susan. *Alger Hiss and the Battle for History.* New Haven, CT: Yale University Press, 2009.

Johnson, Haynes. *The Age of Anxiety: McCarthyism to Terrorism.* New York: Harcourt, 2005.

Lichtenstein, Nelson. *State of the Union: A Century of American Labor.* New Brunswick, NJ: Princeton University Press, 2003.

Mandelbaum, Seymour J. *The Social Setting of Intolerance: The Know-Nothings, the Red Scare, and McCarthyism.* Glenview, IL: Scott, Foresman, 1964.

McCarthy, Joseph. *McCarthyism: The Fight for America.* New York: Devin-Adair, 1952.

Morgan, Ted. *Reds: McCarthyism in Twentieth-Century America.* New York: Random House, 2003.

Oshinsky, David M. *A Conspiracy So Immense: The World of Joe McCarthy.* New York: Free Press, 1983.

Powers, Richard Gid. *Not Without Honor: The History of American Anticommunism.* New York: Free Press, 1995.

Schrecker, Ellen. *The Age of McCarthyism: A Brief History with Documents.* Boston: St. Martin's Press, 1994.

Schrecker, Ellen. *Many Are the Crimes: McCarthyism in America.* Boston: Little, Brown, 1998.

Schrecker, Ellen. *No Ivory Tower: McCarthyism and the Universities.* New York: Oxford University Press, 1986.

Whitfield, Stephen J. *The Culture of the Cold War.* Baltimore: Johns Hopkins University Press, 1990.

Wicker, Tom. *Shooting Star: The Brief Arc of Joe McCarthy.* New York: Harcourt, 2006.

Periodicals

Beinart, Peter. "The New McCarthyism." *The Daily Beast,* September 12, 2010. Available online at http://www.thedailybeast.com/blogs-and-stories/2010-09-12/new-mccarthyism-palin-gingrich-and-us-paranoid-politics/2/.

Goldberg, Jonah. "Two Cheers for 'McCarthyism'?" *National Review,* February 23, 2003. Available online at http://www.nationalreview.com/articles/206038/two-cheers-mccarthyism/jonah-goldberg.

Goldstein, Robert Justin. "Prelude to McCarthyism: The Making of a Blacklist." *Prologue,* Fall 2006.

Kalven, Jamie. "At War with the First Amendment." *Bulletin of the Atomic Scientists,* January 1989.

Shafer, Jack. "*Good Night, and Good Luck* and Bad History." *Slate,* October 5, 2005. Available online at http://www.slate.com/id/2127595/.

Stone, Geoffrey R. "Free Speech in the Age of McCarthy: A Cautionary Tale." *California Law Review,* October 2005.

Online Resources

Appleton Public Library. "Joseph McCarthy: Selected Resources." Available online at http://www.apl.org/history/mccarthy/index.html.

C-SPAN.org. "The Army-McCarthy Hearings." Available online at http://www.c-span.org/special/mccarthy.asp.

University of Missouri–Kansas City School of Law. "Famous Trials: The Alger Hiss Trials, 1949-1950." Available online at http://www.law.umkc.edu/faculty/projects/ftrials/hiss/hiss.html.

Wisconsin Historical Society. "McCarthyism, Korea, and the Cold War." Available online at http://www.wisconsinhistory.org/turningpoints/tp-039/.

PHOTO AND ILLUSTRATION CREDITS

INDEX